Marksm

by David Co

Other works by the author:

The Soldier Chronicles series
Liberty or Death
Heart of Oak
Blood on the Snow

Marksman

Sunlight speared the Spanish countryside, dazzling everything beneath an azure sky liberated of cloud.

To the north, was Valdecarros, a peaceful place of harvested fields, rich vineyards, white- painted farms with terracotta roofs and bright-red poppies. A winding stream, coiling itself in the grassy uplands around the hamlet like a snake, was suddenly spoilt by a galloping horseman that burst out of a grove of silver-trunked corks, splattering quicksilver water over parched soil. The rider tugged hard on the reins and jabbed steel spurs into the beast's chestnut flanks, pricking the tough hide with quick desperate prods of his heel.

Despite the intense heat, he wore a plain grey frock coat over white, long-legged breeches. A sword sheathed in a black scabbard hung at his left hip and his knee-high leather boots were stained with dust and grime.

Captain Steven Kyte of his most Britannic Majesty's Army, raced down the slope towards Valdecarros, his coat undone exposing a heavily sweat-stained white shirt underneath.

'We can't stop, old boy,' he said breathlessly to his mount. 'When we reach Navales, I'll have you watered and stabled like a king that dotes on his favourite nag.' He glanced over his shoulder at the hills, and then down to the village. Blond hair matted his sweat-lined face. He would follow the swirling cool waters all the way to Alba de Tormes where his contact waited for him. The town was only part garrisoned by the French having been taken in the previous year after Spanish troops were routed by superior French cavalry on the banks of the River Tormes. 'You've damn well earned it. Just a bit more to go and we're free,' he said, angling his horse down through a copse of stunted trees. 'Just a bit more, old boy.' His horse stumbled, and Kyte was almost swept out of the saddle, having only just managed to hold on. 'Steady!' he said, trying to soothe the beast, 'steady does it.' The horse, hot foam dripping from the bit and flanks stinking of sweat, took Kyte towards the hamlet. It wasn't much of a place; a dozen houses, a tavern and a small white-painted church that blessed the vista.

A potter, making beautiful intricate tiles under the shade of a wisteria, gaped up at the stranger, before frowning because he had lost his concentration. Kyte edged his horse down the tiny dirt road. Washing hung between the buildings. Vivid colours of field marigolds, wild lavender and asphodels bloomed in gardens, where the infectious and vivifying sound of children played.

'*Inglés*,' he said to the smattering of suspicious glances from the folk who watched him from shadowed doorways and windows. '*Soy Inglés*,' he repeated. It was not good to be French, especially a lone French rider in this war-ravaged land. The guerrilleros stalked them and captured them, tortured and killed them. They were bitter enemies and the French would die a slow and horrible death.

The tavern's door opened with a creak. Dust motes billowed outside. A woman, with hair the colour of black pepper carrying a basket, came to him and he paid silver for a loaf, a length of smoked sausage, bread, tomatoes and a wineskin.

'*Gracias,*' he said and the woman dipped her head to him. Kyte glanced behind again, but no one followed. The enemy was gone and he breathed a sigh of relief, taking in the air of fried sardines and spices wafting from the nearest house. He clicked his tired horse in the shade and a bow-legged man, with a head of silver wiry hair, showed him a trough where water sparkled.

As his horse slurped noisily, Kyte slumped against a kinked trunk of a carob tree, allowing a sudden breeze to stir his ruffled clothes. He was exhausted; having ridden for days, but as the minutes ticked away, he knew the dangers of indolence.

He had a secret and it could not wait.

Kyte hungrily bit into the tomatoes, guzzled the wine, tore at the bread and looped the sausage around his saddle's pommel for later. He had eaten like an animal, but he was too famished to care who saw him. He hadn't eaten anything for three days. His captors had left him with nothing except cuts, bruises and cracked bones. Kyte ran a sleeve across his mouth afterwards, and gazed up at the road where only a cat hunted in a small garden of tangled brown grass.

Two old men chatted beside a collection of penned white guinea fowl. There were no enemies. His mount had finished drinking and he knew that the next part of the journey would be even more uncomfortable, for every stop made it worse. Still, he contemplated; he had out-thought his imprisoners and soon would be free. He wearily climbed up into the saddle and urged the beast on.

Kyte tentatively edged out from the huddle of houses, cool shadows replaced by fiery heat before gazing up at the southern crest. It was wondrously peaceful. A gentle breeze rippled crops and nudged the pale leave of the olive groves and prickly pears. No dust rising from the straggling roads that betrayed movement. He clicked the beast on.

Then, there was a sudden flash of silver in the cork orchard and Kyte's heart raced like a hunted animal's. He fished in his sabretache and pulled out his telescope. He extended the brass tube and scanned for enemies. A nerve twitched along his jaw.

Glints of metal revealed dark shapes emerging from the tree line. Green-coated killers with yellow facings and brass horse-hair plumed helmets on big war horses.

French cavalry. Dragoons.

'Oh God,' he uttered.

The French word for dragoon was *dragon* and Kyte's body shook with nerves as though he had actually seen a mythical beast. They were here! He wiped the sweat that dripped to sting his blue eyes and trained his glass on the leading files. There were at least eighty of them. He could see moustached faces, grim under peaked helmets. Their *cadenettes*; pigtails that marked them as elite, swayed to the stride of the horses. Reflected sunlight glimmered like tiny sparks on their buckles and stirrups. These days the dragoons had taken to wearing cloth covers over their helmets, hoping to hide the gleam of brass and so make it easier to surprise the partisans who they hunted. They carried straight-bladed swords and their short-barrelled muskets were kept in a saddle-boot for quick and easy skirmishing.

He searched for a man dressed in civilian clothes. That was the one he feared. His heart pounded and blood seemed to pop in his ears. He wasn't there. Good. No wait. He searched again. There was a man with a brown jacket. Kyte swore. He was here! Kyte watched the man stare down into the valley where his gaze seemed to wander to exactly where Kyte now waited. The enemy halted. Kyte remained motionless. The man yawned, stretched out his arms and slowly as though he knew the Englishman was watching him, pulled out his firearm from the bucket holster. Kyte's eyes jumped to the walls, fields and to where the sails of a tower wind mill creaked. It was a long way from the dragoons. No musket could ever hope to reach that distance, but the man in civilian clothes did not carry a smoothbore weapon; instead, he carried a rifle: a British-made Baker rifle.

Kyte watched the man who had turned to the dragoon officer to talk. He could see their mouths opening and closing. They didn't seem to be in a hurry or concerned about anything. Kyte looked down at the windmill, back at the trees again and decided to take advantage of the distance. He collapsed the scope, put it back in the sabretache, and kicked his heels back. He felt naked and unprotected as he galloped down through the fields. He twisted in the saddle to look up at the skyline, imaging threatening silhouettes coming, but no one came. The freshening wind blew his hair back as the beast took him with great speed to the structure. From there, he would use the terrain to his advantage, and get to Navales before sunset. A friendly band of patriots patrolled this stretch of land and even a full troop of French dragoons would still be a target for their ambushes, and hit and run tactics. The French invaders held the majority of the towns and cities, but they had never conquered the countryside. There, the guerrilleros were the true victors. They roamed the land like undaunted princes and kings.

'Faster! Faster!' he urged his mount.

Kyte nudged the horse with his knees which indicated where he desired to go and the horse instantly obeyed. He swept past the wind mill, where two women dressed in black gaped at him, and up a slight rise where lizards scurried clear of the thundering hooves. Curiosity made him glance over his shoulder again. The dragoons had not moved, not even attempted to pursue him. What the hell? He gently eased back on the reins to slow down. What game were they playing at? Then, the civilian dismounted and knelt in front of the others. The bastard was about to shoot him in the back.

Kyte witnessed a puff of smoke just before an echo tore through the air. Birds panicked up from the nearest trees, then circled and flew back to the branches as the powder-smoke dissipated. No lead ball struck him. He was alive! The rifle could not reach him and he would not die today! He would complete his mission and this man would be doomed. He tugged back on the reins and gave a huge exultant cry. His horse whinnied and rose up its hind legs. If Kyte had kept his bicorn hat, he would have given an ironic salute.

'Good riddance, you bastards! See you in hell!'

He stayed there for a moment, savouring the feeling of freedom. Then, a second puff erupted from the enemy line. This time, the echo sounded like the crack of a whip and the bullet punched its way through his body with enough force to jerk him clean out of the saddle. Kyte was thrown onto his back. His horse, frightened by the gunshot, galloped off. There was just enough time for him to realise the first shot had been a ruse and the second was from the feared rifle.

He let out a moan and blood vented his mouth to spatter his chin. Everything swirled and he suddenly felt a coldness creep into his shattered body before the world went dark.

****

'Welcome to Navales, *senõr*,' said a quick voice in accented English.

A tall British officer, wearing a blue jacket of the Ordnance, pulled his cocked hat down more tightly to shield his eyes from the molten gold sun. 'Thank you,' he replied, not looking at the man, but gazing up at the thickening crowd of Spanish onlookers. *Like they were watching a damned play*, he thought. One, on horseback, watched the wagons approach with a baleful expression. Another was kneeling down to a small wayside shrine with his back to them. *Some reception.* 'Is this Navales?'

'*Senõr?*'

'We're a day late. Our guide got us lost and then, the rascal promptly disappeared.' The miserable officer waved the olive-skinned Spaniard away with a flick of his wrist. 'Probably on purpose. Never mind. This must be it.' He sighed and gazed up at the shuttered white-washed houses, the crop fields that edged all the way to the horizon, the suspicious townsfolk and grimaced at the dark-skinned children hardly clothed at all and crawling with lice. He shuddered with distaste.

'May we look at the guns, *senõr?*' the Spaniard asked politely.

The officer clicked his fingers and a group of privates unfurled the canvasses on two thick-wheeled wagons. There were muskets and pistols, barrels and crates of ammunition and powder. A half-dozen mules, tethered to the rear wagon, carried more firearms and a private stood sullenly holding the officer's mount.

Captain George Israel Cotton reached inside his newly-brushed jacket, dragged out a red handkerchief and mopped his brow. His buttons and badges gleamed. 'I must say that the journey was atrocious. The roads here are either in poor condition or completely non-existent. I suppose you fellows don't know how to build them. No skills and all that. The weather must have something to do with it. I was supplied a map, but God knows what for. The hills on this drawing show them to be to the north, but in reality they are to the west. I don't know who is to blame. The cartographer, or the Almighty for creating such a strenuous and wicked country.'

'*Senõr?*' the Spaniard asked, baffled at the whining Englishman.

'Nevertheless, I'm here to present the guns to a,' Cotton paused to read his orders, 'Colonel Antonio Herrero.' He gave the mounted one an inquisitive glance, and wondered when he would have the nerve to ask the Spaniard to sign the papers for the receipt of the arms.

The Spanish, at the behest of the mounted one, began to take the weapons until a voice called out. It was almost guttural. They all turned to the man who had been praying at the shrine. He had long coal-black hair, turned grey at the temples, and tied back with a bow. He wore a moustache in the typical Spanish fashion. He was unshaven with a hard angled face that bordered leanness. They watched him descend the heather-haunted slope to the wagons where he picked up a musket and cocked it. He shook his head, threw the firearm down, smoke-coloured eyes scanning over the rest of the weapons.

'Rust,' the man said, holding another one up. 'Goddamned rust.' He shot Cotton a look of menace.

'I say...' Cotton started, but the man's belligerent expression was so brutal that he failed to finish what he was about to say.

The guerrillero continued to manhandle the muskets. He lifted one up, shouldered it and aimed it squarely at Cotton who blanched.

The dog-head snapped forward with a loud click. The man tossed the weapon onto the pile. 'It won't do. It won't do at all.' In and amongst the stacks of muskets of all ages and conditions were carbines, ancient muskets, musketoons and even snaphances. 'This isn't what was promised.'

Cotton adjusted his bicorn. 'Who are you, sir?' he said in the tone of one trying to acquire self-respect in the face of absolute insolence.

The man ignored him. 'Firing plates missing, loose triggers, fouled barrels, missing flints, missing screws, missing mainsprings...' He paused whilst he picked up a smaller firearm, seemingly taken away with it.

'That's a rifle,' Cotton said. 'Made by gun-maker Ezekiel Baker, and was selected by the Board of Ordnance for The Corps of Experimental Riflemen in 1800.'

'I know what it is,' the guerrillero snapped. He ran a hand up and down the barrel, and then down to the stock, fingers feeling the grain of wood like a lovers caress.

The Baker rifle had seven rectangular grooves in the barrel, which gave it its deadly accuracy because it spun the ball when fired. Like the German Jäger rifles, it had a scrolled brass trigger-guard to help ensure a firm grip and a raised cheek-piece on the left-hand side of the butt for snug purchase. It also had a patchbox located in the rifle's brass bound butt where the Rifleman would keep greased linen patches, a cleaning kit and tools. In short, it was a beautiful weapon of lethal precision.

'Is this the only one? A pity. It will do, but only suitable for parts. The rest...' Cadoc shrugged. 'Not worth the bother. What are we supposed to do with them? Some of the stocks are infested with woodworm. I haven't checked the powder and cartridges yet, but I'm guessing they're in a sorry state too. Now, you can take them all back to your depot and return with complete working muskets, oiled, polished and with flints.'

'I..er-'

'I want the guns back here in three weeks. No later. And this time I want a score of rifles and our riders need good horse shoes. Britain makes the bloody best and I want a five hundred brought back with you.' He rapped on the lid of a trunk half-hidden by arms. 'What's in here?'

Cotton's eyes bulged at the demands. As the red mist of outrage passed, this amounted to him stomping a leather boot into the ground and grinding his teeth, he suddenly realised the man had been speaking fluent English, but with a Welsh accent. Cotton eyed up the man's appearance with this new knowledge. He wore a pair of brown leather half-boots and heavily patched dark green pantaloons the same colour as his jacket and a black leather belt with a bayonet frog that was wrinkled from harsh weather. One or two white-metal buttons were missing on the coat, replaced with bone or white-painted wood, but there was no mistaking the black cuffs and delicate white piping.

'What are you doing here, Rifleman?' Cotton exclaimed, face leering. 'Deserter, are we? I can have you shot for that.' The captain's men looked over with eager attentiveness.

The guerrillero let the silence drag as he looked back at the shrine.

'I asked you a question, damn your insolence,' Cotton's nostrils flared. 'As a captain of His Majesty's Ordnance, I order you to-'

The patriot turned and grabbed Cotton by the lapels, shoving him back against the wagon before he could utter a gasp. His black felt bicorn tumbled down over a shoulder.

'You don't give me orders,' the partisan said. 'Now, you've a job to do, so get your arse moving.'

Seeing his commander being jostled, a huge lantern-jawed corporal shouldered his way through the throng, drawing a muscled arm back. The partisan, seeing the threat, ducked as the thick-fingered fist harmlessly punched the air. He nimbly dodged the next attack and brought up his right fist, which caught the corporal clean under the chin, knocking him backwards into Cotton who made a sound like a bagpipe being squeezed. The moustached man swiftly followed it with a right jab, a left, and then a right. The NCO shook his head to clear it from the assault, but was too slow to stop a thump to his belly and a powerful uppercut that knocked him clean out.

Cotton stood wide-eyed with the corporal groaning and bleeding at his feet. The guerrillero had a mask of someone used to gutter fights and brawls that wouldn't be out of place at a dockside tavern. Cotton's legs buckled slightly.

12

The NCO gasped and twitched back into consciousness. Blood seeped into the dry soil from a cut above his right eye. He stared disorientated, tried to move his limbs, and failed.

'Are you all right, Corporal?' Cotton managed to ask.

The NCO blinked and looked up at his assailant who had not moved.

'You get up again, boy, and we'll have another go,' the guerrillero told him.

The corporal hesitated, thought better of it, and held up a hand in submission.

'W-who are you?' Cotton gaped.

The man adjusted the rifle to stare up at the tall captain. 'Arthur Cadoc,' he said, 'and I was once a Chosen Man of the 95th Rifles.'

****

Cadoc was twenty-nine years old and from Fishguard, Pembrokeshire. He was the eldest son of six generations of fishermen who lived in a tiny house near the cove's harbour. He had first fought the French during the invasion of his town, February 1797, aged sixteen. The French, on-board a ship flying a Union Flag, had deceived the local yeomanry who let them disembark thinking they were comrades. Cadoc had found out their plans and alerted the militia and a skirmish ensued. Adept at hitting target with slings and with his father's old fowling piece, Cadoc killed six French soldiers with a yeomanry carbine. Praised for his shooting skills, he was convinced that his talents lie elsewhere rather than fishing for the rest of his life. He enlisted in the Light Company of the 43rd Monmouthshire Regiment, and then through skill, joined The Corps of Experimental Riflemen three years later.

'So you've been soldiering for a while now,' Cotton said.

Cadoc was a dangerous-looking man. He reminded Cotton of the other campaigners: men as tough as old boots and he was a Welshman; a born fighter, and a proper warrior. He had knocked out Leatherby in seconds. Cotton had seen the raging fire in his eyes, the intense look of a prize-fighter and a champion of knuckle fights. The captain adjusted his neck tie. He was twenty-five and had bought his captaincy after the British victory at Talavera, and had never seen

13

action. The two of them were now seated and shaded under a thick canopy of wisteria vines that ran across a trellis outside the village's tavern. Wine, cheese, figs, bread and ham were served on plates. If it wasn't for the war, it could have been a blessed day in paradise.

The Rifleman merely grunted a reply and speared a cut of the meat with a knife, putting a thick piece into his mouth.

Cotton, feeling awkward by the confrontation and the fact that he did not know how to converse with the rank and file, shifted in his chair. He'd given his men permission to smoke and brew tea at the wagons, and that had at least been received with a satisfactory grunt from Leatherby. 'So, where have you seen action...?' His voice faded because he did not know how to address the Rifleman-cum-guerrillero. His stomach rumbled painfully, but he was too timid to take some of the food.

Cadoc watched a bee buzz between the beautiful purple flowers overhead as he chewed noisily. 'Copenhagen, Roliça, Vimeiro and Corunna.'

Cotton tried to hide his embarrassment from the green-jacket who had accomplished feats he could only dream of, and exuded competence, by casting his gaze down at his boots. A scarlet glow flooded his hollow cheeks. 'Copenhagen?'

Cadoc, apparently oblivious to the captain's misery, bobbed his head. 'Aye, peculiar bloody fight that was.'

'What happened?'

The Welshman picked a strand of meat from between two teeth with a finger. 'We landed, fired a few volleys and left. It was something to do with the Danish fleet. Strange, like I said. Same thing with Buenos Aires.'

'What in God's name were you doing there?'

Cadoc stroked the ends of his moustache. 'I haven't a clue. I was a soldier. I was sent there. I never asked any questions.'

Britain had sent an expeditionary force under General John Whitelocke to seize some of Spain's territories. It proved to be disastrous and after suffering heavy losses, the army had surrendered. It was a humiliating defeat and upon returning home Whitelocke was court martialled and cashiered.

'We could have fought on, but the general had us surrender,' Cadoc continued unhappily. 'General Craufurd was there and he said to me if I was to see the general I was to shoot him.' The Rifleman

14

suddenly laughed at the memory. 'It's not the first time I've shot a bad officer. But this time I wasn't so lucky. My aim was off and the general lived.'

Cotton didn't know whether to believe the tale, so he grimaced, before glancing over to where his men waited with the parked wagons, stiff with bristling stoicism. The Spaniards seemed pleasant enough and looked content to smoke pipes, drink and talk amongst themselves. There were about thirty of them. Only the mounted one looked out of place. He was as hard-looking as Cadoc, same height, but more refined with a long aquiline nose and a carefully trimmed moustache. He was well-dressed in a short scarlet jacket, with dark curls and his cheeks were widened with bushy side-whiskers. His brown eyes met Cotton's, and yet, there was no acknowledgement. The captain considered that his presence was not wanted, so he would leave after taking refreshment.

'Corunna,' Cotton said, 'now that was a sad affair.'

'You were there?'

'No, but my commanding officer was in one of the last ships to set sail after the battle. He was there when they buried Moore.'

Sir John Moore, the commanding officer of a small expeditionary army, had been sent to Spain to sever the invading French supply lines. The French, who had pounded half of Europe, turned on Moore who, after a series of Spanish defeats that left the British alone, was forced to retreat through the Galician mountains to Corunna. There, they had to do battle in order to allow the men to embark on the waiting transport ships. The British, following their fighting retreat, were victorious, but Moore was killed in the final stages of the battle. It was a terrible loss to the army.

'I lost three toes to frostbite, nearly a finger, and was severely wounded in the battle,' Cadoc said, remembering that every day was another tortuous march of cramped bellies, pain and cold. 'In fact, a local doctor said I was at death's door and would not be able to travel. I didn't want to stay here. I thought once we landed, I would have been transported to Hilsea where the regiment has a hospital. But upon hearing that Sir John had died I wept like a babe.'

Cotton had heard of Sir John's reputation as an inspirational leader for having pushed the boundaries of new light infantry tactics, and of the national grieving that followed his death. 'By all accounts, you were lucky to survive.'

'Aye, I thought the retreat would kill me for sure. It killed one of my best friends. But we're a tough lot: us boys from the 95th. First on the field and always the last off,' Cadoc said proudly, scratching at the scar on his belly where a musket ball had nearly killed him.

Cotton knew of the Rifles status. In the decade since the regiment's early formation, it had won the admiration of every veteran battalion in the army. They were considered the elite.

'What happened to you after Corunna?'

Grazia. That was what happened after the retreat. He closed his eyes, because the image of her was strongest then. Beautiful Grazia, with her dark tousled hair, snow-white teeth, and slender body. He missed her. 'I was nursed back to health. I was dreadfully thin and my hair had turned grey. But I lived. The fleet had sailed home without me. I was stranded.'

Cotton still couldn't understand why the Welshman hadn't tried to re-join the army since his recovery. 'Is that why you became one of these bandits?'

'They are decent men,' Cadoc riposted. 'Not all guerrilleros are scum. These help the locals rather than intimidate and rob. They report enemy movements to our intelligence too. Spy for them. They do good work. Work that will help turf the bastard Frogs out of this country.'

Cotton reddened from the rebuke. The stories he had heard of their acts of vengeance on the French had left him in a cold sweat. It was strange to hear something respectable about them.

Rather than apologise, he said something else. 'So do you lead these men? Or is it left to that patriot on the horse?'

'Colonel Antonio Rai Herrero,' Cadoc chided him. 'He's a fine gentleman.'

Cotton wrinkled his nose at the gentle reproof, considering that he deserved it for being boorish. He sighed. 'He looks a bit brutish if you ask me.'

Cadoc grunted with mirth. 'You have to be to fight this war. Rai has seen tragedy. His home was burned down and his wife and children thrown to the flames by the French. Now he hunts them.'

'Dear God,' Cotton could only say.

'After the ships had gone home, nobody knew where our boys would be sent next. Some said Lisbon. Some said they were going to the Netherlands. By that time the whole north was crawling with the bloody French. So I decided to throw my lot in with them.'

Cotton narrowed his gaze. 'Was it because of the girl?'

Cadoc's eyes twinkled with the memories. 'You're a perceptive sod, if you don't mind me saying so. Yes. Her brother was a guerrillero. I spent much of '09 with them.' He remembered the savage attacks on the French, the ambushes, the raids, the sabotage and the torture of prisoners. The exhilaration, terror, anxiety and the horror of his new employment haunted his dreams. But not as much as Grazia's death, or her brother's at the hands of the vengeful French. Cadoc managed to escape the slaughter to drift down into the plains where he stumbled onto a skirmish between Rai's men and a Polish Lancer troop. He picked off all the officers with his prized rifle and the lancers retreated. Rai begged him to fight alongside his men and he accepted. 'But I'm here now.'

'For good?'

Cadoc smiled, his teeth flashed brilliantly in contrast to his sun-darkened face. 'I'm happy here.'

'What about your regiment?'

And that was the truth of it. Cadoc did miss his old comrades. He didn't know who had survived the battle of Corunna and where they were now. He was proud of the Rifles and what they had achieved, but would he be welcomed back? Would the Provosts come looking for him? If he was found guilty of desertion, then he would be hanged for sure.

Cotton continued seeing Cadoc's hesitation. 'You still wear your old coat.'

Cadoc nodded vehemently. 'With pride.'

'Even though you've turned your back on your regiment?' Cotton saw the Welshman's expression darken. 'What I'm trying to say is that even as a guerrillero you still wear your Rifle uniform.'

'I'll be buried in it too.'

Cotton slapped away a fly, frowning. The tiny insects seemed to multiply with every minute of the day. 'Where are your loyalties, Cadoc? I don't understand.'

Cadoc had wondered the same thing since Corunna. But he had helped the locals riding with Rai's group and he was highly thought of. Rai was a good leader and an honest man and although Cadoc's Spanish wasn't very good, he could communicate well enough with

17

them. Besides, he didn't miss the constant orders, the marching, the peacock-strutting officers, vindictive NCOs and definitely the rations. Out here, he had at least found freedom. But he still missed his old friends, their coarse humour and the larking about. By wearing his green coat, he thought himself still part of them; perhaps they wouldn't forget him as he would never forget them.

'I'm still killing Frenchman, and so I'll stick around and help these people out. When the bloody Frogs are defeated, I'll think again about what to do, or where to go.'

'Return home?'

Cadoc shrugged. 'Maybe.'

'A bit different than Wales, eh?'

Cadoc chuckled. 'I miss the green hills. I miss the rain. It rains here, but it isn't the same stuff. I miss the valleys and the woods. Aye, you probably think I'm a sentimental fool.'

'I miss home too,' Cotton said. He pursed his lips, sweat glistened on his top lip. He rattled fingers on the table as though he was anxious. 'When I turn in my report, I'm going to have to tell my superiors about you.'

Cadoc leaned back in the chair and blinked.

'My dear fellow, I have to,' Cotton replied earnestly when there was no reply. 'I have to tell them that your men refused the weapons. That'll send ripples into the pond. Ripples will cause waves and the top echelon will want to know what happened. They always do. Perhaps Lord Wellington of Talavera will hear about you? Nothing escapes his ear, so they say, and I know for I have a cousin in the Staff Corps.'

'That's a shame.'

'I'm sorry?' Cotton said, straightening himself.

'No, I'm the one that's sorry.'

Cotton lifted his eyebrows suspiciously, but remained silent as the Welshman spoke.

'You, your men and your wagons aren't going anywhere.'

The young officer jumped out of his seat, bare head knocking a cluster of the hanging wisteria. 'What the deuce? How dare you threaten-' he bellowed and Cadoc waved a dismissive hand.

'You don't understand, Captain,' he clarified. 'You're staying put, because we're going to kill the Frogs, and you're going to help us.'

Cotton took a gulp of air.

****

'The firearms aren't just for us,' Cadoc explained to the young officer, 'they are meant for an uprising.'

'After Bailén,' Herrero said in a tone of cold civility, 'it told the world that the French could be defeated and that the Spanish would not lie down like dogs and be forced into submission. It proved that we can fight,' he paused to drink from a wineskin. 'It proved to you *ingleses* that we can fight and it spat in the face of the devil, Bonaparte.' He spat out the emperor's name as though it were a piece of rotten meat.

Bailén had been a resounding defeat for the French two years ago. Their army tried to break through the city having been outflanked and driven back. Following this, they capitulated to the Spanish, losing eighteen thousand as prisoners of war. The victory spread like wildfire across Europe and it seemed that the French would be expelled, but the Spanish armies were no more, the government hid in Cádiz and Napoleon had installed his brother Joseph, as King José-Napoleon I of Spain.

Cotton shot a worried glance at the wagons. He knew the arms were old, rusted and no good. Any uprising with these weapons would be short-lived, but he dared not reveal that sentiment. His commanding officer, Major Edeson, a burly Yorkshireman, had chided him for his concern.

'They are only for the irregulars, Cotton,' he had answered back at the tiny depot on Portugal's border. 'Damned bandits with no morals and ideals. They care not for their people or for Spain's future, mark my words. They care about killing, looting and raping. No discipline, see? The Dons can't match the Frogs in the field and so all that's left for them to do is bite and sting like bloody gnats. Let them take the arms, and report back to me by sun down. I have something more important for you than cleaning out our stock piles. It seems the Frogs have sent an army to take Portugal. And so what remains of us here will pull back behind the Lines.'

Cotton had heard about the Lines of Torres Vedras, which were a series of redoubts, blockhouses and ravelins strategically placed on

19

the top of hills and passes outside Lisbon. The forts were defended with artillery batteries, militia and regular troops. Below: the land was completely destroyed and turned into a huge glacis. Every ounce of food had been removed or burned, vineyards cut down, and wells were filled with stones or fouled with carcasses, livestock taken and homes demolished. The French, who famously lived off the land, would have nothing to supply them. In essence, they would starve.

Edeson scratched at an insect bite on his buttocks. 'So all Monsewer Bonaparte has to do is take Portugal. The dagoes have been beaten, the Austrians and Russians out of the war, Prussians dithering, which means only us left to beat.'

Cotton had ignored the major's summation of the emperor's strategy. 'What happens if they refuse the arms, sir?' he had said.

Edeson had looked galled at the prospect. 'The devil take the ungrateful wretches!'

Cotton stared at the scarlet-coated officer. 'How can I possibly help you? I work in the Ordnance. My job is deliveries, stores, sometimes repairs. Drudgery.'

'Exactly the man we need,' Cadoc said.

This assignment is getting worse, Cotton said to himself. He gazed around, uneasy.

Rai ran long fingers through his luxuriant black hair. 'You want to kill Frenchmen, Captain?'

'Yes, they're my enemies too.'

Rai watched him like a hawk watching prey. 'I am a colonel in the Spanish Army, Captain. I would appreciate the courtesy given to my rank.'

Cotton could see no evidence of this on Rai's clothes, only taking a stranger's word on the matter. Besides, where was Herrero's regiment? Where were his men? His red jacket was modestly plain, patched on one elbow and he wore brown woollen pantaloons, stockings and *alpartarga* sandals. The only evidence of him being an officer was a battered officer's bicorn of a Spanish line regiment, and Cotton had seen several guerrilleros wear the same headdress. They all carried the *cuchillo*; a Spanish knife, pistols and muskets. Nevertheless, instinct, and what the Rifleman had said, told him to be respectful.

'Of course, sir,' he replied politely. 'I apologise for my incivility.'

Rai gave a tight smile, pleased that he had made his point, but did not revel in the reproach. 'I want the French expunged from my country. And to make that a reality, Captain, I have to kill every Frenchmen I see. By any means.' He leaned in closer to Cotton. He brought up a cigarillo and puffed a couple of times, the blue smoke drifted away with the breeze. 'Ever since the scum killed my wife and my children, I have hunted them. I am good at it. I specialise in it. And for those I capture I kill. Eventually.' He gave Cotton a wolfish grin. 'I have cut them in places that would make you sick. I have plucked out organs whilst they still breathed. I have burned them. I have shot them. I have strangled them and I've even drowned them. If it had not been for the deceit of the French, we Spanish would still be your enemies. It is not too long after Trafalgar, no? But fate has brought us together, and so together we will drive them back across the Pyrenees to their hellish cesspits where they belong. You can play a part in this, or simply walk away. Your choice.'

Cotton licked his lips. However inexperienced, he would not be called a coward. *From the pan into the fire.*

'I'll stay, sir.'

Rai watched him for a moment, before nodding. '*Bueno.*'

'I've got something to show you,' Cadoc said with a twitch of a smile, and tying back a black bandana in the customary partisan fashion. 'And bring your boys too. They'll need to see what we have up here. That corporal's a strapping lad, isn't he? A proper brawler that one.'

Leatherby was the biggest man Cotton had ever known, and hitherto, Cadoc had knocked him out in seconds. Somehow, he considered, bulk had nothing to do with winning a fight.

'Quite,' Cotton muttered laconically.

Cadoc and Rai led the seven blue-coated men to a huge stone barn situated on the rocky crest above the town. The doors were pulled open and inside were great hillocks of hay. Cadoc went over to one of the mounds and hauled at the dried grass. At first, Cotton thought the Riflemen had lost his wits, but then he caught a glimpse of metal, and suddenly there was a wheel and carriage.

'One of them is Spanish, two are French and there's one of ours here too,' Cadoc said.

Cotton looked stern. 'You brought us up here to help drag them out?'

21

'No, Captain, much more than that,' Rai was smiling. 'You're going to fix them.'

'Fix them?' Cotton gaped at the old clumsy pieces covered in dust.

Cadoc slapped the barrel of the nearest one. 'I believe this is a Spanish twelve pounder. Sebastiano says it is a siege gun. The carriage is split. So one charge and it's done for.'

Cotton, enthused by the different cannon, inspected it carefully. He saw the two cracks in the carriage, which had been damaged in an accident. His eyes scanned the bolts, fixings and screws. 'This piece has different wheels, which tells me they've been replaced by limber ones and not refitted. And you see underneath the barrel placement there are severe dents. The left trunnion is buckled. This one was dropped, or slid down onto rocks. Most likely because of the treacherously narrow roads that seem to frequent this country,' he said, a smile playing on his lips, saw Rai's expression and then stared with serious determination. 'It's seen some action, though, from the apparent scorch marks around the muzzle.'

'What else can you tell me about it?'

'Well, this Sebastiano, you mentioned, is wrong. This wasn't a siege gun, or for garrison use because it would be red or stained with black fittings. Spanish carriage colours of the year of this one's manufacture were blue-grey, so this was a field gun. The pigment they used in the paint was actually cobalt blue; derived from cobalt oxide and, when it was exposed to the weather for a long period of time, it had a tendency to fade to a wishy-washy grey. I've seen this before.' He looked at the barrel, running a hand down from the swell, the neck to the vent. 'The good news is that it can be fixed. You need a team to lift the barrel in order for a carpenter to mend the carriage. A wright should be able to sort out the trunnion, and it does need its iron fittings replaced too. A bit of work, but it could be done.'

Cadoc raised a black eyebrow at the captain's knowledge. 'I'm impressed. Now tell me what you know of these two Frenchies.'

Cotton caressed the two cannons, crouching and looming over them. 'The first one is an old four pounder. I can't see the mark, so I'm guessing forty years old? It's got a wooden axle, not an iron one, and the barrel is cracked.'

'What does that mean?'

'It means it's useless.' Cotton gawked at the second one, teeth gnawing his upper lip. 'This is a heavier piece, an eight pounder. Looks sturdy, except it has no wheels,' he said wryly. 'Barrel is clean. Carriage is firm. Should be able to get this one to work.' He examined the last one. 'This is a British six pounder. Iron barrel painted black to protect it from rust. It worked, to some degree, but the vent is blocked. It's possibly been spiked.' This meant that the gun team, or an enemy, had driven a barbed metal spike down the touch-hole to prevent the cannon from being used again. With great skill, the spike could be drilled out, if not, it was beyond repair. 'I'd also need to see what's in the chamber. That too could be blocked. So you have two guns, possibly three, at your disposal.'

Cadoc grinned widely at Rai who gave Cotton a curt nod in appreciation.

'Seems we may have your guns fixed now, *senõr*,' Cadoc said to the Spaniard.

'*Bueno*,' clapped Rai. 'I am very pleased. This will help ensure that the French will regret what they started.'

But just as the men celebrated, a voice called out a warning. There were frantic hoof beats coming from the west.

Rai raced to the doorway and an urgent message was relayed to him from the town's courtyard.

'What is it?' Cotton asked Cadoc, panic clear in his voice.

The Rifleman checked that his rifle was loaded. 'No. Our scouts have brought back a uniformed man from the plains.'

'French?'

'No,' Cadoc replied. 'English. And a friend.'

****

Kyte was barely alive.

He still breathed, but would die soon. There was nothing more to be done. Navales' doctor, Duilio Escarrà, had probed for the bullet, but he could not locate it. The gun shot was too severe, and Kyte had simply lost too much blood. Escarrà muttered something as he washed his bloody fingers in a bowl. He cleaned his instruments and washed out his bleeding-cup; coagulated gore floated on the surface.

'What did he say? It sounded like he said catholic?' Cotton asked, craning over Kyte's form. The small room was heated by a fire, and because of the midday sun, Cotton found himself sweating profusely.

'Doctor Escarrà said another heathen protestant dead in a catholic land,' Cadoc explained, holding up Kyte's long coat to examine the bullet wound. It was sodden with blood around a ragged vent.

Cotton could feel sweat dripping down his back. 'Who is he?' he said, gazing at the dying man.

Rai had been praying silently; clasping onto one of Kyte's hands tightly as though God could heal him, got up from his knees. In his other hand, he held rosary beads. 'His name is Steven Kyte, and is a friend to me and my brother. He has helped us countless times. And now,' Rai, face contorted with emotion and voice thickening, 'he will die.'

'Captain Kyte worked in the Peninsular Corps of Guides as an Exploring Officer,' Cadoc revealed.

'What does that entail?' Cotton asked.

'Kyte had a network of contacts throughout the area and provided information on Frenchie troop movements, where they went, were going, how many of them, infantry, cavalry and guns. He knew the colonel here very well and he knew the land. He always rode in uniform, so that he would not be accused of being a spy, but it looks like someone captured him.'

'How can you tell?'

Cadoc stooped and raised one of Kyte's wrists, showing red welts. 'He was tied up. There are also marks on his neck. Strangulation marks.'

Cotton stared wide-eyed. 'You mean to tell me that Captain Kyte was tortured?'

'Yes.'

'My God! By whom?'

Cadoc gaped at the man's naivety. 'By the French of course!'

Cotton looked as though he wanted to sit down. 'B-but they're our enemies.'

'Yes?'

Cotton rubbed his face. 'But,' he paused, 'there are rules of war. Wasn't Kyte given parole? He's an officer, for God's sake. A gentleman. Gentlemen don't go around tormenting each other like that.'

Rai looked appalled, and then sighed despondently. 'You English are so naive. This is war. This is horror. At Évora, the French massacred men, women and children. They pillaged, they raped and they tortured civilians. That's right, Captain. They raped women and children. Young infants. Blood ran like streams and the screams of the violated echoed to the next village. Priests were bayoneted and nailed to doors. Church silver stolen. Men had their eyes gouged out and were butchered like winter hogs.'

'My God,' Cotton said softly, looking as though he wanted to weep.

'The French are men with no honour. They come straight from the devil's own backside.'

'Look sir, we need your help,' Cadoc said to Cotton. 'We need those guns working so we can slaughter the bastards and maybe the ones that did this.'

Kyte jerked awake. His face was greyish, his skin slick with sweat, his eyes crimson- rimmed, and he began to mutter incoherently. Escarrà spoke hurried Spanish to Rai.

'What did he say?' Cotton asked Cadoc, the heat prickling sweat on his cheeks.

'He says that Kyte has a fever. His mind is gone. We'll never know who did this to him.'

Rai took his hand again. 'Steven, my friend,' he spoke in English because he wanted Cotton to understand. 'We shall ride again someday. A day under a glorious Spanish sun that is free from all enemies.' Cotton thought he saw the Spaniard glance sideways at him. 'I will pray for your soul. *Adiós, amigo.*'

Escarrà grunted. 'He won't understand you,' he said in rather good English that surprised Cotton. 'I wish I could offer more hope, but there is none. Allow him to enter God's realm in peace. I shall bring in Padre Tos. He can give our friend what he needs now.'

Kyte whispered something and Rai went closer to the bed. 'Steven? I didn't hear you? What did you say?'

Kyte's eyes flickered, stayed on Cotton who stared aghast, rolled like a tormented beast and finally closed.

'He'll not make any sense,' Escarrà stubbornly insisted. 'I did warn you.'

'He just did,' Rai responded quickly. 'He said *colaboracionista*.'

Cotton gaped at the grim faces in the room. 'What does that mean?'

Cadoc was solemn. 'It means betrayer.'

****

Chef-de-battalion Pierre Helterlin had a journey of nearly one hundred and fifty miles and had to be escorted by a squadron of his dragoons who clattered across the border and into the Portuguese city of Pombal long after nightfall. He climbed wearily from his mount, handed his helmet to an orderly, and limped to the house where a tricolour flew proudly. Orange trees grew outside and the citrus scents teased his nostrils as he climbed the steps to the grand building. Ten sentries stood outside, their muskets tipped with bayonets that reflected the lights from inside.

Helterlin climbed the stairs, nudging his sore thighs with a gloved hand. He took a step towards the central door and pounded on it. Sounds of muffled voices came from inside, floorboards creaked and the door was opened by a smartly dressed orderly. Several men in a brightly lit room were engaged in conversation, drinking wine and smoking cigars. A blazing hearth fire gave off a ferocious blast of heat.

A man wearing an intricate patch over one eye frowned at Helterlin 'Who the hell are you?' he asked coldly.

Helterlin cleared his throat and was interrupted by a tall man with a shock of red hair who appeared beside One-Eye.

'This is the man I was telling you about, your Highness,' De Marin said in flowery tones.

Marshal André Masséna, Duke of Rivoli and Prince of Essling, the commander of the *l'Armee de Portugal*, grunted and gulped back brandy.

Helterlin felt everyone's gaze upon him, and Masséna's seemed to be boring itself into his very soul. Sweat began to sheet his back. 'Your Highness,' he said, bowing awkwardly, which prompted a snort of laughter from the marshal.

Masséna beckoned him closer with a hand, eye traversing over the man's stained and weather-worn uniform. He had lost the other

26

eye in a shooting accident while hunting with the emperor, and, ever since, had worn a patch.

'*Chef-de-battalion* Helterlin fought at Jena–Auerstedt and Preussisch-Eylau, and received the *Légion d'Honneur* because of his heroism. He is a man much like yourself, your Highness,' De Marin said. 'Capable. Resourceful. He commands-'

Masséna waved a hand in disinterest. He gazed back at the handsome dragoon officer who had blond hair and the palest eyes he had ever seen, so faintly grey as to be almost transparent. 'I just need to know if you can do the job. Are you the right man?'

Helterlin had no idea what he was being required to do and was reluctant to admit that, but nodded anyway. 'Absolutely, your Highness.'

'Good.' The marshal sucked on a cigar. 'You understand what you have to do and what,' he paused to consider his words, 'that might entail. You won't be popular, that's for sure. In fact, you will have a bounty on your head. Can you live with that? Yes? Good. Know that the guerrilleros will likely come after you. But being popular doesn't mean you'll win battles. This is war. War is brutal. Horrid.' He leant closer to Helterlin and jabbed a finger, painfully, into his chest. 'Just make sure you are more horrid than the peasants. You'll earn respect that way. You'll be feared. And with fear, we'll win this damn war before Christmas. Remember: adversity brings knowledge and knowledge brings wisdom.'

Helterlin looked at De Marin for support, but the red-headed man was beaming widely as though he was in awe of the Marshal. The dragoon officer considered there was only one reply he could give.

'I'm the man for the job. I'll see it completed. You have my word, your Highness.'

'You see,' De Marin said, patting Helterlin on the shoulder like a proud father.

Masséna sniffed at the remark and drew on the cigar, eye narrowed as it sought to discover if the dragoon was correct. There were so many young officers trying to prove their worth. He understood ambition. He had fought his way up through the ranks demonstrating merit. He was decorated and given the title of Marshal. The emperor even called him *l'Enfant chéri de la Victoire*, the Dear Child of Victory. Masséna knew reputation was everything in life. Men had to prove ability first.

'Have you eaten?'

'Not yet, your Highness.'

'There is some cold chicken and bread. Plenty of wine. Eat and drink and then I want you leaving for the border by dawn.'

Helterlin bowed. 'Thank you, your Highness.'

Masséna grunted and walked away to refill his brandy glass.

Helterlin's eyes quickly surveyed the scene hoping to catch a glimpse of his mistress who reputedly dressed as a dragoon officer, but she was not here. *Probably waiting in their bed*, he surmised with a smirk.

'Your mission is simple,' De Marin said, watching the marshal's retreating back. He turned sharply to Helterlin. 'What I'm about to tell you is strictly kept within these walls. Understood? You are to kill several partisan leaders before they increase their numbers. They will flee and scatter, and then we will destroy them. I shall provide you with their names and where they operate. If we are to be successful here in Portugal, we need our supply lines free from attack. I need men like you to make that happen.'

'Yes, sir. And thank you for considering me.'

De Marin's gaze became steely. 'I'm giving you a second chance. After the apprehension of the English spy, you were given strict instructions to acquire names of those who work for them. Alas, you did not.'

Helterlin swallowed. 'He proved to be very stubborn, sir. My methods of extracting-'

'You failed and that is the answer,' De Marin cut him short. 'I ordered you to escort him to me and it is deeply unfortunate that he escaped. We had one of Wellington's Intelligence officers, only to lose him from our grasp. Your grasp.'

'I apologise again, sir,' Helterlin's face burned. 'I corrected the grievous error before he could warn anyone.'

De Marin said nothing for a while. 'A pity.'

Helterlin didn't know if De Marin was saddened by the death or by the fact that he did not acquire contacts from the Englishman.

'The first name on your list is a Spaniard by the name of Herrero,' De Marin said. 'His men are being armed by the English. I want you to strike now and run the quarry to ground. Exterminate them; all of them.'

'Sir.'

De Marin inched closer. 'No more mistakes. Complete your mission and redeem yourself. Perhaps, you'll even get promoted. I know you seek advancement. That's why I chose you. I like men who are hungry for success. Bear in mind thousands of others are equally eager to make a name for themselves. I am not sentimental. If you die, you will be replaced. Earn it, don't lose it.'

Masséna, chicken leg in hand, came over as De Marin finished what he was saying.

'Are your men ready?'

'Yes, your Highness.'

The marshal bit into the succulent meat. 'Do they know how to fight?' he said, half-mocking.

'Yes, your Highness. And they know how to kill too,' Helterlin crowed.

'Very good. I like you, Helterlin. There's something about you dragoons that I like. Not the ablest horsemen in the army; not like the Hussars or the Chasseurs-à-Cheval. But you fight with unquestionable pluck, and I like that.'

'And he has help, your Highness,' De Marin said.

'Oh? You perhaps?' Masséna said, and Helterlin noticed a sneer in the tone.

De Marin gave another beaming smile. 'I very much doubt I can offer assistance to our gallant *chef-de-battalion*. No, I was referring to another,' he pursed his lips before continuing, 'eager recruit.'

'My man carries a rifle. He is an expert shot, your Highness.'

Masséna considered the answer and spat a lump of gristle onto the floor. 'Rifle? I've no time for them. Too cumbersome to load. Like trying to undress a fat whore.' He laughed at his own joke. De Marin chortled and shot Helterlin a look that he had better join in.

The *chef-de-battalion* joined in with the mirth. 'A marksman, your Highness, who will shoot the heads' off every partisan leader in Spain.'

Masséna laughed at the boast. 'Good and if that's the case, you shall be a *général de brigade* by the time we take Lisbon.' He thumped Helterlin's arm playfully, before joining the group of officers seated by the fire.

'Good, he likes you. Smoke this Herrero from his den,' De Marin spoke softly and intently. 'Kill him and fulfil your destiny.'

A smile creased Helterlin's face. 'I will, sir. You can count on me.'

****

Steven Kyte died as Escarrà predicted. The Englishman had clung onto life, but by the second day, he slipped away without a sound.

The sky at dusk was violet and the western clouds glimmered gold. And as the air cooled and mosquitoes hunted, more guerrilleros came to Navales.

The dozen men, dismounted, and tethered their horses at the stable. Cotton watched from the abandoned house opposite that Cadoc had said was theirs for the night. The tiled roof had partially collapsed and the windows weren't shuttered, but the men from the Ordnance had been given a delicious hare stew, wine and two loaves of fresh bread. The partisans saw Cotton's silhouette, and then with suspicious glances, entered the tavern. One remained with the horses. Cotton saw smoke pluming from a clay pipe and a tiny smear of lit tobacco lighting the man's moustached face framed by a large wide-brimmed hat.

Cotton, naturally inquisitive, left Corporal Leatherby in charge of the men whilst he ventured towards the tavern. He had washed his hands and face, brushed his coat and wore his blue coat buttoned up. He was a British officer and as such, it was imperative to be smartly dressed at all times. He was nervous, but wanted to know what news had the guerrilleros brought of the French. And, he cogitated, as a captain fighting the same enemy, it was his right to know.

He turned right into the alley when three of the new Spaniards appeared with muskets pointed at him.

'Lower your weapons. I am Captain George Cotton-'

One with a yellow coat and brown pantaloons stepped towards him. '*Inglés?* You look like a Frenchman.' Cotton licked his lips. 'I kill Frenchmen,' the Spaniard continued, gesturing with a hand drawn slowly across his neck like a knife.

Cotton could smell his stale tobacco breath from six feet away. 'Good for you,' he managed to say despite the fact that he was trembling.

The guerrillero spat. 'I have no love for you *ingleses* either.'

'I don't care who you are or where you are from,' said the tallest of the three. He had a gravelly voice, and a face decimated by the pox. 'But you should know that I'm the best knife-fighter throughout Spain.'

Sweat beaded Cotton's forehead. 'No doubt you spawned that rubbish yourself.'

Pox Face hissed, like a lit powder fuse. '*Inglés!* Give us your money!'

Cotton looked exasperated. 'You…you are robbing me?'

The Spaniards came closer. 'Are you deaf? Yes, we are. *Tonto del culo!*' They laughed mockingly.

'But we're allies?' Cotton wanted to back away, to flee in sudden fear. And he would have done if his right hand had not automatically reached for the sword sheathed at his left hip, and pulled it free effortlessly. The sound of it reverberated loudly in the small space.

The guerrilleros seemed undaunted by the threat, and merely laughed with contempt. 'You think you can touch us with that? *Que te jodan!*' Pox-Face stepped forward, his ravaged face breaking into a snarl. 'I'm going to stick that in your heart! You *ingleses* are gutless dogs! *Te voy a matar!* I'm going to murder you, Englishman!'

'No, you're not,' said a voice to his left.

The Spaniard swivelled his face in time to see a fist hurtle out of the shadows. The punch was powerful enough to knock out his front teeth and to send him crashing into his comrades.

Cadoc gave the other men no chance to stand. The first one to react was kicked in the ribs as he drew a pistol from his belt. The kick was massive, but he held onto the firearm. Cadoc slapped it away with his left hand to send it skidding into the shadows and then stamped down onto the guerrillero's face, feeling bone snap. The third Spaniard, entangled with the first one, was trying to draw his sword when Cadoc swung one of their muskets as a club and the heavy stock connected with his temple. Cotton thought he saw a mist of crimson in the gathering twilight as the man was flung violently back.

'This one's always trouble,' Cadoc prodded Pox-Face, who groaned through the new gaps in his teeth.

Cotton grimaced at the twitching, bleeding men. After a moment, he found his tongue. 'Thank you.'

Cadoc rubbed his blood-stained knuckles on one of the Spaniard's coats. 'You can put your sword away now,' he said with a grin. Shadow and light danced across his face.

Cotton, gripping his weapon tight like a dead man's final grasp, rammed it home. 'T-thank you,' he said, stammering. 'I-I was just...I was going to...to...'

The Welshman, realising the captain was in shock, led him away by the elbow to the tavern. 'What you need right now is a drink. A proper one. That'll set you right.'

'That wasn't very gentlemanly,' Cotton said of the attack.

Cadoc gazed over the bodies. 'No, it wasn't. And if you fight like one, you'll be on the ground spitting blood before you can say 'oh bugger',' he mocked in a well-spoken English accent. 'You fight hard and fight dirty. That's the only way to do it.'

'I think I need to return to my quarters. I suddenly miss it.'

'Drink first,' Cadoc said, pushing the tavern's door open and into the warm fug of tobacco, and blazing hearth fire. The rich smell of spices and oil from the kitchen made their noses twitch.

Rai was drinking at a table with another man. They both looked up.

'Is something the matter, Rifleman?' It was the first time Cotton had heard the colonel use that title.

Cadoc took a squat bottle off a table, wiped the rim with his grubby sleeve, and gave it to Cotton. It was *aguadiente*: Spanish brandy. 'Drink up.' He turned to his commander. 'Paz is up to his usual tricks. This time he threatened the captain and tried to rob him.

Rai looked livid and the man opposite him slammed a fist down onto the table. He got up and strode over to Cotton, thrusting a calloused hand into his. He saw that his right cheek was pock-marked with powder burns, his almond eyes were bright with intelligence. He wore a long brown cloak of homespun, draped over a shoulder. Cotton considered they all had brown woollen garments because the Spanish sheep had dark wool, which didn't need dyeing.

'My name is Adolfo, but my friends call me Fito. I apologise for this, *senõr*. This is not how we treat our allies. I shall deal with him immediately.'

Paz, one of Fito's men, had been an outlaw with his brother, but they were caught by the French and his brother was hung. Paz managed to escape to join Fito's men and it is said he carved every

32

kill into his musket's stock as a grim reminder. He was a troublemaker and Fito only allowed him into his partisan band because of his hatred for the French.

Cadoc drank from a wineskin. 'I gave him a tickle. He won't try that again.'

'Usually, I discipline my own men, but on this occasion I hope you did more than that?' Fito gave the Welshman an almost reptilian smile.

Cadoc had only ever met Fito once before and didn't take to him then. He was guarded, suspicious and standoffish, and was nothing like his brother who was cherished by the locals. Cadoc had seen women and men; tough creatures from the mountains, kiss Rai's hand in awe. They adored him. Fito was a cold fish, and Cadoc sensed a hunger in the man that was more than provisions. He wanted power. He wanted to be a general in the army, but he was not a Don, or wealthy enough, so became a partisan instead.

Cotton gaped at Cadoc's flippant remark. 'You did more than tickle the surly brute. I've...I've never seen anything like it.' He could not get the image of the fight from his mind. Cadoc had simply despatched them in seconds, sparing him from a rare beating, or worse. He gulped back the brandy and tried not to let it show that he found it too eye-wateringly harsh.

'My Rifleman does have unique talents,' Rai put in.

'So I hear,' Fito said, nodding with approval. He had the same eyes as his brother, but that was where the similarities stopped. It was difficult to discern age from a face heavily-lined around the eyes and mouth where there was a thick, pointed beard at his chin. Cadoc guessed Fito was in his late thirties. He carried a sword and a pistol and one of the long Spanish knives at his side.

'What is the name your men call the Rifles?' Rai directed the question to Cadoc.

'Green jackets, *senŏr.*'

'Green jacket,' Fito said the word as though it was new to him, and smiled to indicate he liked it.

'Who'd have thought that enemies could become friends,' Rai happily puffed on a cigar.

'Come on, let's drink,' Cadoc said jauntily. He rose a brandy-filled cup. 'Success to grey hairs, but bad luck to white locks!' He repeated the ridiculing toast made following General Whitelocke's cowardice at Buenos Aires.

The Spaniards frowned at the unusual saying, but nevertheless repeated it in accented English and drank.

Rai beckoned them all closer. 'Let us talk.'

****

Fito had ridden down the plains from Salamanca, avoiding many French cavalry patrols. 'It is infested with the scum,' he said. 'There are not enough bullets in the world to kill all of them, or enough of our countrymen to pull the triggers.'

'You talk nonsense, *hermano*,' Rai chided him playfully.

Fito laughed and puffed on a cigar. 'It's true. I have seen them with my own eyes. They still come in their thousands across the mountains. Their supply lines stretch longer than the Tormes.'

'That will be their undoing. They need a full corps to protect it. All the while we buzz about them like wasps after jam; killing their officers, intercepting their messages, diverting wagons and capturing their weapons and ammunition.'

'The guerrilla way, eh?' Fito grinned.

Rai bobbed his head. 'Always, *hermano*. We raid, kill, flee and survive to fight another day.'

'And wear out our boots if nothing else,' Fito said with a laugh.

'I will never tend a vine or again plough the field until the French are driven from all of Spain.' Rai's expression took on a solemn tone. 'Captain Steven Kyte was brought here today. He was found outside Valdecarros. He had been shot.'

Fito's eyes went wide with shock. '*Dios mio*. Dead?'

'He did not live long.'

'Who was responsible? The French?' Fito crossed himself.

Rai shrugged. 'I'm not sure. The only word he spoke of was *colaboracionista*.'

Fito gazed into his brother's eyes, into Cadoc's and finally Cotton's. 'Who was he talking about?'

'We don't know,' Rai said. 'He said nothing more.'

Fito drank from the wineskin and puffed on his cigar. 'I have heard of an *afrancesado* west of Salamanca, near the border. El

Medico searches for him.' El Medico, The Doctor, was another partisan leader who operated in La Mancha, but his band had grown to hundreds and now watched the hills and plains around Madrid, Salamanca, Avila, Segovia and Cuenca. 'As of yet, the French-lover has not been caught. But El Medico will find him and strip the skin from his bones when he does. Perhaps our friend Steven found out his identity?'

'And killed him because of that,' Rai breathed.

'Rope burns and cuts indicated that he had been a prisoner,' Cadoc added. 'I knew Captain Kyte well enough and he would have used every trick to break free and escape.'

'We must find those responsible and punish them,' Fito angrily declared. He stood up quickly and Rai ushered him down with a hand.

'What are you doing?' he said. 'Sit down. You have ridden hard to get here. Your men are tired and there is much to talk about. We have other news to share.'

'Every *afrancesado* and *colaboracionista* must be stopped if we are to see King Fernando on the throne again. Spanish lives depend on this. Gossip can wait.' Fito hurried to the door and beckoned his men to join him. He turned back to his brother. 'In five days come to our safe place in the caves,' he said. 'I will be there. We will talk. *Adiós.*'

Cadoc watched the retreating men. Paz and the two others climbed groggily and bleeding into their saddles and then they were gone into the night.

'What on earth was that all about?' Cotton said to no one in particular.

'Forgive my brother,' Rai said. 'He has never forgiven the French for the murder of my wife and children. He loved them like they were his own. Now Fito builds up his guerrilleros and soon we shall number two hundred. Now,' he said, banging the table with a palm. 'We must avenge Steven. Let us drink! *Viva* Fernando VIII! To our friends! And death to the cursed French!'

****

Firelight flickered through the trees to the east of Navales.

'No, fires, Juan! The colonel will roast our backsides if he finds out!'

The Spaniard called Juan stamped out the fire, scattering cinders and sending sparks into the night air. 'I'm goddamn cold!' He cursed and shivered, pulling his cloak around his body.

'You should have pissed on it,' said his companion. 'It would have been easier and less noisy.'

Juan puffed on his cigar. 'You would have me piss on a naked flame? Are you out of your mind? You know I've been drinking *aguadiente*. One drop, and I would have exploded.'

The two men laughed and resumed their watch. The moon was full and they observed the plains and roads for enemies.

Behind them, dark shapes shifted and slithered in the gloom.

****

If Cadoc hadn't gone outside to relieve himself he would never have seen a dull glint on the wooded crest that dipped all the way to the roadside. He dressed himself, staring at the dots of light. He rubbed his eyes, his clothes stinking of tobacco and alcohol, as the shadows melded into the forms of men. Scores of them approached the town like a gathering wolfpack. He ran back inside.

He kicked the door open, which slammed into the wall, grabbed his rifle, yelling a warning to the dozen men still awake. 'The French are here! Get up! Get your weapons!' He knocked out a lantern on one of the tables as the men roused. 'Extinguish the lights!'

A volley of loose musketry rattled the walls, splintered glass and three Spaniards were thrown bloodily back. Plates of beans and cups of wine clattered onto the floor. The serving girls screamed, except one wearing a red flowing skirt, who picked up a fallen musket and calmly approached a shattered window.

'Get down, Edita!' Rai shouted, as he tugged his pistol free from the belt. 'Down!'

Edita, a twenty-year-old with dark curls and a playful grin, shouldered the weapon as any good soldier, and pulled the trigger. Scraps of flaming powder debris singed her right cheek, but she did not twitch. Cadoc saw a shape fall. Then, there was movement to his right, a Frenchman aimed at her, but Cadoc edged his rifle barrel

36

through the window and, using the wooden frame to steady it, shot the man dead.

Rai's men extinguished the last of the lanterns, overturned tables and fired through the windows, the weapons belching smoke that stank of rotten eggs. One or two hesitated, wondering where the best spot for cover was and Rai leapt up, grabbed their arms and shoved them forward.

'I want fire! I want fire!' Rai ordered.

The Spaniards poured fire through the windows. One, wearing a sky-blue jacket of a Spanish Light infantry regiment, vomited because he was half-drunk, and then reloaded soberly.

Cadoc saw that Edita had wrenched free a cartridge holder from one of the dead men and was loading. He smiled with approval and a smile tugged her lips. Rai had given him Kyte's telescope as a present and now he trained the glass to the woods. He could see grim faces, muskets and swords. He assumed they were French Voltigeurs, but he saw Grecian helmets and long black horsehair crests twisting with every motion behind them.

'They're bloody golden-heads!' Cadoc used the Spanish nickname for French dragoons.

'How many are there?' Edita asked.

'Perhaps a company strong, senõr,' Cadoc said, closing the scope. He pulled out a cartridge from his belt, bit an end off with the ball, pulled the hammer to half-cock, flipped open the pan and poured a pinch of powder into it. Then, the rest went down the muzzle with the paper as wadding. He spat the ball down after that and drew his ramrod. He could hear bullets whip in the air.

'Infantry?'

'I didn't see, or hear any horse,' he replied, thrusting the charge home with his ramrod.

'What are they doing here?'

'Trying to kill us,' Cadoc said glibly. He pulled back the rifle's hammer to full-cock.

The French were spread thinly as they struggled to control all of the many villages and towns. There was no garrison of brigade size for twenty miles, and these men were braving the night when partisans liked to stalk. No Frenchmen left their forts unless they were sure of success or led by men that feared nothing. But he wondered whether the French were nervous of being in Spain and

Portugal, always watching over their shoulders, never sure if the enemy lurked in the shadows and if so, how many of them were there. He was glad he was not a Frenchman.

Carbines blasted at the tavern. The crash of so many incoming shots let loose in such a confined space was near deafening, and Cadoc could barely hear his own voice. He gawked at the walls. It would be dangerous to leave, but he did not know how many men waited for them out there in the darkness. To stay here, trapped, enemy bullets whittling them down one by one and chewing at their morale was a death sentence.

'We can't stay here.'

'My thoughts exactly. We don't know how many of them are here or if others are on their way.' Rai looked grim. His men did not live in the village. They had no formal home of their own preferring to live in the hills, gullies, caves and abandoned farmsteads. He did not want the folk here hurt because the guerrilleros stayed there. And after the attack now, they would not come back again. 'I need to see if Sebastiano, or Ciro have got our men from the homes. I wonder what happened to my men in the woods.'

Cadoc tap-loaded the rifle by thumping the stock against the floor, instead of using the cumbersome steel ramrod. It saved time, but reduced the rifle's firepower. 'Likely they are dead, *senõr*.'

Rai grunted because he had been thinking the same. More French lives his *cuchillo* would take in revenge. 'What about the captain?' He had to shout the last sentence as another volley crashed into the room. Jugs were smashed and bottles fell to the stone floor. A bullet slammed through the window and struck one of the beams above Cadoc's head.

There was no light coming from Cotton's tiny quarters. Cadoc wondered if he had left a guard stationed near the door who had seen the attackers and they had taken precautions. Otherwise, the French, taking the sleeping British as Spaniards, would likely kill them where they huddled. He hoped Cotton would remain unmolested, or not do anything stupid. He liked the young man. There was a spark of bitterness when he first saw him. Cotton was the spitting image of a lieutenant from the 43rd who had made Cadoc's early life misery and the Rifleman thought Eurion Prothro had returned to haunt him again.

The French were shouting, '*Vive l'empereur!*' It sounded mocking, as though it would easily strengthen their victory. Cadoc knew that the dragoons were extremely loyal to the emperor, their cause and would carry out their orders to the last man. This would be no easy fight.

'We can't worry about him now, *senõr*,' Cadoc yelled over the sound of gunfire, taking aim at a grey shape and the rifle bullet took the man through his neck. 'I'm going to circle the town and go up to the barn. I need ammunition, so I'll go get my pack first and return. Up there will give me an advantage. I can see where the bastards are going.'

The Rifleman was gambling on instinct that the dragoons were attacking en masse in the hope of surprising their enemy, rather than assailing multiple points. He stared out where moustached faces with their odd pigtails fired back. He thought he could hear a Rifle bugle signalling the order to 'fire and retire', but he realised he was hearing things from days long gone past.

'Very well, *amigo*. I will regroup our men. Take Niguel with you. He's a good shot too.'

Cadoc glanced at the young man behind the colonel who had eyes that burned with a keening anger, but he turned to Edita who had already loaded and fired again. 'I'll take her.'

****

'Come on, girl. Let's make some mischief.'

The two of them snuck out of the tavern's tap room and into the yard where the owner kept goats and mules. Cadoc slipped on fresh dung, but managed to keep upright. He edged to the stone wall. There were no enemies lurking in the shadows, or hiding at the alleys and he guessed that the French had not hitherto reached this far into the village. He tap-loaded the rifle again and tugged free his long sword-bayonet to slot it onto the muzzle. His dark green coat was black in the half-light, which gave the riflemen the nickname 'sweeps', because they looked like chimney-sweeps. There was another blast of musketry coming from the trees. Cadoc tugged Edita's sleeve and she followed him as he sprinted down the road. He saw a figure lurch by the wall of the nearest house, blood showed

39

on his white shirt and then there were shadows with long blades behind him. Somewhere a dog barked incessantly. Cadoc pushed the girl down. The Spaniard collapsed as the blades did their death work. A moustached face below a peaked helmet laughed.

'You Toad bastard!' Cadoc snarled. The rifle flamed bright, and in the flash, he saw three Frenchman twisting aside as the bullet struck the laughing one in the chest to send him backwards.

There was no time to load and he stepped back as the dragoons rushed at him, steel flashing in the moonlight. The first one didn't see Edita and her musket took his life instantly. The next dragoon hesitated because there were now two enemies, one a man who looked in half-shadow and a beautiful Spanish girl's face contorted into something bestial. And because of the hesitation Cadoc took the advantage by charging with his sword-bayonet. He was screaming incoherently as the twenty-three inch blade, honed razor-sharp ripped in between the man's ribs. He twisted the blade free, the alleyway stank of blood. The last dragoon, wearing brown homespun overalls, brought up his short-barrelled musket, pointing the muzzle at Edita.

'Look out!' Cadoc threw himself at her, knocking her over as the musket banged above them in an orange burst. The ball sang harmlessly overhead.

The dragoon threw it down, unsheathed his sword and sprang forward. He thrust the blade down, aiming at Cadoc's heart, but the Rifleman kicked his assailant's knee and the dragoon went off balance. The blade speared Cadoc's flank, ripping into his coat and slicing just below his hip.

The Frenchman swore at him as Cadoc grabbed hold of his collar. 'You're not going anywhere, you ugly bugger.'

Edita leapt up and grabbed hold of the dragoon's face by his forehead and cut his throat with a knife that gleamed silver before turning crimson in the blink of an eye.

Cadoc was sprayed with the hot blood. He heaved off the jerking, gurgling body. 'Good girl.'

'Are you hurt?' she said in English.

His fingers probed the cut; they came stickily away. It was deep, however, there was nothing he could do about that now. He cut a strip of cloth from a dead dragoon and tied it around the wound. 'I'll be fine, love,' he said, wiping his face with a ragged sleeve. 'Let's go. We have work to do.'

They scurried through an orchard of lemon and lime trees and up to where the road touched the first houses. The musket fire was still sporadic, which told Cadoc the French had not given up, or that Rai's men had not been defeated. Opposite the house was the shrine where he had first encountered Cotton and his wagons. He checked for enemies first, then satisfied they were alone, led Edita up there.

Her brows arched, bridging bewildered eyes. 'Are you going to pray now?' she sneered. 'Rai told me you were just another godless protestant.'

Cadoc scrambled up the slope to the shrine of Teresa of Ávila, a Saint who stayed in the village on her journey to Salamanca. It is said the villagers were struck down with an illness, and she found they were under a devil's spell. She located the creature in a cave and destroyed it with holy water, and thus saving the souls of Navales. Cadoc got down on his knees and shoved aside the statue of the Saint and baskets of flowers.

A dog padded its way down the roadside, seemingly obvious to the sound of gunfire. Goats bleated in one of the fields and a vixen cried somewhere. The rich smell of animal dung mixed with the roiling gunpowder made Cadoc's eyes water.

'What are you doing?' Edita said angrily. 'This is sacrilege!'

Cadoc ignored her, pulling at something from deep with the shrine's niche. 'If I don't get what's in here, there will be blasphemy of a kind you've never heard the likes of before, girl.' He gritted his teeth, then his fingers found grip and he dragged out something heavy. Edita continued gaping at him.

'Here they are,' he said, bringing forth a pack of sorts and a belted box.

It was his infantry pack and black leather cartridge box, which contained his readymade cartridges. The box was issued with a wooden block inner that was designed to hold twenty-four cartridges. Each one contained a patched ball and a measured amount of gunpowder wrapped in greased paper to be used as wadding so the ball stayed in the barrel. Most Riflemen used the holders as kindling, preferring to have up to twice as much loose and the added weight. During the retreat to Corunna, the men had as much ammunition crammed into their packs, because of the worry of

41

supply problems, but they discarded spare boots, shirts, box of blacking and shaving kits to keep the rounds. He had a score of gold napoleons hidden in the pack as well as another twelve stitched into his coat, all taken from French corpses. The pack, rifle and clothes on his back were everything that he owned in the world.

Unique to the Rifles was the powder horn. It was made from cow's horn, fitted with a number of brass spouts for measuring precise charges of gun powder and contained fine ground gunpowder that gave a greater accuracy. It was usually suspended from the cartridge box cross belt by a length of green cord that allowed it to be moved easily from its carrying position on top of the cartridge box to the Rifleman's front for loading.

'Why did you put it in there?' Edita asked, jutting her head at the shrine.

Cadoc flashed a roguish grin. 'No one would think twice to look there, now would they? There is a pistol in the bag and sixty rounds. Check it's loaded and load your weapons too.' There was sufficient light to load, but after years of training, he could load a firearm blindfolded.

When it was done, they snuck up to the barn, treading over the dry, pale heather that teased his nostrils with its warm scents. Cadoc went first, Edita trailed him. They heard the sound of rats scrabbling away. He edged along the side of the building, and, happy that no enemies lurked, went inside. He propped his rifle, pack and cross belt against the stone wall and moved two squat barrels to the entrance where he could steady the rifle's barrel against them and use them for additional cover.

'Keep the pistols and musket close by, just in case any of the bastards come up here,' he said, removing the bayonet because it made the rifle unbalanced.

'*Sí*.' She gave him an inquisitive glance. 'You have killed many men?'

He nodded. 'Aye.'

'You are a good shot?'

'The best,' he said with a grin.

She seemed pleased with that answer. 'Then, you will kill more tonight. That is good.'

Cadoc stared down to the village. Weapons flared and shots rang out. He could see Spaniards firing from the church doorway and

42

windows. Flames flickered in the night air. From what he could comprehend, was that the French had now stormed the nearest houses, including the tavern, but had been checked by Rai's men. He remembered he now owned a telescope. He had an idea. He gave it to Edita to spot the enemy whilst he adopted a suitable firing position.

The men of the 95th fought ferociously, and were made more deadly because they were trained, unlike other infantry, to fight independently. They would not look to an NCO or officer for instruction as privates would do in the red-coated battalions, but knew, thanks to their training, just exactly what to do. On a battlefield, there were none better. And now, Cadoc, a man bred for war, and trained to be the best of the best, would fight and kill his enemies.

'There are six of them by the stables,' Edita said. 'One is now kneeling, and looks like he's reloading. There are two on the stables roof. There are…four maybe five running to the church. I can see a group trying to break the doors of Doctor Escarrà.' She smiled wickedly when the doctor fired a blunderbuss down into the green-coated men from an upstairs window that left the dragoons twitching and bleeding.

'Tell me if you can see their officers,' Cadoc said, staring down the barrel. 'If I can kill them and the NCOs, the buggers will retreat. Look for dragoons with gold epaulettes, or those that you can see giving orders.'

'It will be difficult in the light, but I will try my best.'

Cadoc risked a glance at her and could not help, but feel his heart pang for such beauty. He knew of Edita, but thought she was being courted by one of Fito's men.

Humberto, known as El Gigante, was six foot eight inches and the biggest man Cadoc had ever seen. It was rumoured that he had caught a French messenger by punching the horse in the face, knocking it out, and then proceeded to twist off the unfortunate man's head with his bare hands. 'There is one in the group around the stables.'

Cadoc trained his rifle down to the stables where enemy dragoons were gazing round corners, firing at unseen targets and loading their muskets.

'He is second from the right,' Edita said helpfully.

43

'Got him,' Cadoc spotted a shimmer of gold on the officer's right shoulder. He was directing the two on the roof when the Rifleman's bullet severed his spine.

'You hit him!' Edita cried out excitedly.

The Welshman was already loading. 'Secret is the patched ball,' he told her. 'It takes a bastard amount of time to load one, but in the right hands the rifle is truly deadly.'

'Like in your hands,' she said, giving him a smile.

'I was the best shot in my company,' he said, 'probably the battalion. Tom Plunkett, a friend of mine, is a crack shot. Back in '07 when we were besieged in a convent by your lot in Buenos Aires, both of us were on the roof picking off every goddamned enemy we could spot. We tallied our kills; over fifty dead before we were ordered down. So what I'm saying, girl, is that tonight I'm going to perform miracles of my own. Now, what are the Frogs doing down there?' He could hear shouting and a bullet ricocheting somewhere.

Edita raised the glass to an eye. There were coats of green everywhere. There were puffs of smoke and she saw a Spaniard tumble out from a window. It looked like Ciro, the shepherd's uncle, dead. 'Two of them are carrying the officer away, but it doesn't look as though the others have noticed us.'

'Good.' He pulled back the hammer to cock the rifle.

Somewhere a man screamed and a dog kept barking frantically, until there was a curse and a sudden harsh bang of a French musket or carbine.

Edita resumed spotting. It had taken Cadoc twenty seconds to load the rifle. The next bullet found a sergeant who was leading a squad towards the road towards the church. The one after entered through the back of a corporal who was aiming at someone in one of the houses. The ball glanced off the stables stone wall, sending a spark into a patch of hay. The corporal slumped as the flames twitched and smoke billowed. Cadoc shot a man trying to climb a ladder, so that he seemed to hang there as blood dripped obscenely down the rungs. The rifle snapped at a dragoon pointing towards the church where it seemed the guerrilleros had made their bastion. The man pitched sideways behind a house, obscuring Edita's vision. She trained the scope down the road, up to Eduardo, the cooper's house, then down to the tavern where her heart quickened. A group of dragoons had noticed the rifle fire. A fearsome- looking officer with an eye-patch pushed five men towards them. They came crouching low.

'They've seen us!' Edita wailed. She was suddenly pale, but that could have easily have been just the moonlight. 'They're coming for us!'

'It's going to be all right, love,' Cadoc said calmly. In truth, he feared being cornered and the French blades would hack and slash their bodies to turn this barn into a butcher's yard. It would be a horrible death. 'Tell me where they are? Use the glass.'

'They are...they are coming up from the tavern in a...a zigzag way,' she said. 'Is that how you say it?'

'I understand,' he said and found them. He held his breath, felt the thrill of power and squeezed the trigger. Almost immediately after the rifle made its distinctive crack-like sound, he tap-loaded.

'One down,' Edita's voice was ominous. 'There is a really tall man. His shoulders are very wide.'

Cadoc brought his weapon up to his bruised shoulder. He found the next target. 'Is he as big as Humberto?' he asked clumsily.

Edita stared at him. 'No,' she muttered. 'Humberto is bigger.'

'Oh right.' He sighed slightly downheartedly. 'Are you two still sweet on each other?'

'No,' she said laconically.

'Good,' Cadoc said with renewed interest, glancing at the Spanish girl who smiled back.

The ball took the big man in the throat as he attempted to weave towards a jutting rock. As he knelt to load, muskets drummed up at the barn.

'They're firing at us!' Edita warned through the glass. She saw three puffs of smoke and heard the sound like buzzing bees as the balls slashed above the grass.

'They haven't the range,' Cadoc said coolly. 'And now they have to load them.'

The French corporal screamed as the flames found his flesh.

The dragoons had stopped to reload, lying on their backs or behind the large rock, but they had not yet warned their comrades of the Rifleman and so Cadoc waited until they showed themselves. The first one looked from behind the rock and fired up towards the barn, as another decided to clamber up the slope. Cadoc had expected the diversion, and the bullet spun the Frenchman backwards in a cloud of scarlet.

'Three left,' Edita said.

'If they charge now, I won't have enough time to fire again,' he warned.

Edita could see three shapes, like creatures coming from the earth, coming towards them. She snarled at their bravery. 'They will be here soon.'

Cadoc's eyes went to the musket. 'Grab the pistols and wait here by the other barrels. When they come in, take your shot.' He reached over for the heavier firearm and cocked it. It was smoothbore and would never hit a target more than seventy-five yards away and could be inaccurate at fifty.

But the dragoons had assumed that the marksman had been alone and was a guerrillero. They never thought that a British Rifleman could be the culprit.

'*Vive l'Empereur!*'

The dragoons charged. The musket spat fire to send the ball through the officer's remaining eye. He was lifted clean off his feet, sword flashed bright as it skittered down the slope. The nearest dragoon fired his musket and the bullet went close to Cadoc that he felt its passage like a thump of air. Edita fired the pistols into the nearest dragoon, the first tore into a thigh, the second lodged in his pelvis. He fell to the ground wailing in terrible sobs before Edita calmly slit his throat. The last dragoon's nerve broke, and he turned tail back down the incline yelling and shouting. The rifle ball took him clean through his open mouth moments later.

A trumpet sounded, high and shrill. Cadoc took the glass and scanned across the village. It seemed the dragoons were retreating. Bands of Spaniards emerged from houses, doorways and from behind walls to fire at the enemy.

'We did it!' Edita screamed in joy, planting a kiss on the Welshman's sun-scorched and blackened face. 'Thank God!' She clasped her hands and murmured a rapid prayer.

Cadoc smiled. 'Thank God for the Baker rifle and the Welsh.' The saltpetre from the powder was rank and dry in his mouth. He needed wine. *A pint of it would go down nicely*, he reflected.

The skirmish was over and, as Navales stank of blood and smoke, there were so many unanswered questions.

****

The remnants of the stable still smouldered even though the fires had long been put out before the new day's dawn. A silky brightness spread over the hills, lanced through the branches of the tall oak, chestnut and elms, and laid across the graves like a blanket. The charred remains of the dragoon had been dragged from the ash to be buried with the other twenty-two dead French in a mass grave north of the village. They were in a pile, stripped of all weapons and clothes. Flies blanketed the corpses. Padre Tos, his cassock swirling up dust as he walked had even said a prayer for them, not out of respect, but hoping their ungodly souls would not return to haunt Navales.

'Eleven of my countrymen died here,' Rai lamented. 'Eleven who will never see another Spanish dawn.'

Cadoc was staring at the white-skinned bodies. 'We'll avenge them, *senõr*,' he said, half-grimacing at the blood-letting to come. He wore a black hat favourable with the Spanish infantry over a black bandana. It kept the fierce sun from his eyes, ear and back of his neck.

Rai spat to show that he was eager for retribution. 'Our *cuchillo*'s will soak our hands with French blood.' He fingered a discarded dragoon helmet. A bullet has ripped away a chunk of the canvass that covered the brass as protection and to prevent it from reflecting sunlight to betray the French position. The material was a cheap imitation of leopard skin, denoting it was an officer's headdress. He tossed it away, half-wondering if he should keep it as a memento. 'And you, *amigo*, what magic did you work with your rifle? Edita tells me it was perhaps fourteen or fifteen killed?'

'I wasn't counting.'

'She told me that you were very good with your hands too.'

Cadoc flushed. Images of the girl's naked body whirled about his mind. After the fight, the Spaniards mourned their dead and he and Edita had shared *aguadiente* and harsh cider before pulling off each other's clothes and making wild passionate love. They kissed with so much force that he was sure he had cracked a tooth. They made enough of the glorious sound with the cot creaking loudly to cause

47

gossip. But they did not care who heard them. The horror and excitement and sadness of the fight had burned that night, and so their lovemaking was needed to slake it.

She laid back, back arched as he had given her pleasure and afterwards, she lay with her head resting on his muscled chest, her hair tickling him. But he did not move. He traced a finger up her arm, and down her shoulders along her spine. She moaned with content and kissed his torso. She clasped a hand around his forearm, studying the long red tattoo on his arm.

'What is it?' she had asked.

'The red dragon of Wales.'

She traced a finger down the spiralling tail and scales of the mythical beast that ran down his entire arm. She propped herself up to stare at the beast's armoured body and open maw. There appeared to be letters up and along the dragon's body. She angled her head, pulling back a tousle of dark hair from her eyes.

'What do the words say?'

'*Dihina'r ddraig sy'n cysgu a fydd well ganddoch gael achos l,*' he said and she grinned at the unfamiliar language. 'It roughly means in English 'If you wake the sleeping dragon, you'd better have cause to'.'

'Why did you have it done?'

'The French attacked my home back in '97. They were dressed like British Fencibles and fooled us. But not for long and I had it inked in celebration of us beating them before I joined up.'

'Have the French woke the dragon?'

Cadoc reached down to a wineskin and brought it to his mouth. He offered her a drink: she titled her head back as the liquid squirted down into her open throat.

'Aye, they have, girl. More fool them. And they've stirred a hornet's nest over here too where even God can't help the bastards.'

They drifted off to sleep and he woke to find Edita still slumbering. He dressed and went to the woods opposite the town, where he found the ragged bodies of the two sentries.

'Padre Tos says that God blessed us last night,' Rai continued.

Cadoc chewed the inside of his mouth, thinking that Edita was indeed an angel sent from heaven. 'True, *senõr.*'

'She is a wildcat, *amigo.*'

48

Cadoc didn't know if he was being warned or not. 'She certainly knows how to handle herself. She killed two of them with musket and pistol.'

Rai breathed a sigh of appreciation. 'Our padre said we could kill the 'antichrist' French with God's consent. Every man, woman and child is an enemy of France. They will die to protect it from invaders.'

Cadoc was not a godly man, but respected the views of others, careful not to show his own if they differed. 'We gave the Frenchies a drubbing they'll not forget, *senõr*.'

Rai gave a bitter laugh. 'The bastard French thought that they could walk over us. They thought because our leaders were corrupt and incompetent, they would find its people easy targets. But they underestimated us. They thought as King Fernando and the royalty were gone, our armies scattered like the windblown embers of a fire, that God had abandoned us too. No. He listens to our prayers and blesses us. Last night he showed that miracles do happen.' He gave Cadoc an appreciative look. 'Miracles in the form of a Rifleman. I would never have guessed. I have known you *ingleses* for a number of years. The rankers, dull, ugly men.'

'True,' Cadoc conceded.

'The officers a collection of self-righteous preening idiots.'

Cadoc laughed. 'We call them Jack Puddings.'

'But with you,' he clasped the Rifleman's arm, 'I believe what I have always thought: God sent you to me.'

The Welshman was embarrassed with the praise. 'Thank you, *senõr*.'

'I must admit, she is quite lovely, is she not?'

'Perfect,' Cadoc said, his mind swirling with images of Edita.

Rai mumbled a disagreement. 'I would not say that. I am sure you know the faults of such a thing. After all, you told me you spent many years training with it.'

Cadoc realised that he was talking about the Baker rifle. He ran a dirty finger from the hammer up and along the barrel, which was fouled with black powder. Hot water would clean it out and he would do that shortly. During the lull in combat, it was common to see a man piss down the barrel rather than wait for water to boil.

Cotton emerged sheepishly with his men. They had been spared the attack because Cotton had seen the dragoons coming and had ordered his men into the shadows. The French seeing a lifeless, half-tumbled building did not expect to find anybody in there so left it alone. The captain's decision had saved their lives, but his eyes showed guilt. He saluted Rai and nodded a greeting towards Cadoc. He looked even more remorseful when he saw the bodies.

'I should have helped.'

'There was nothing you could have done.' Rai shot him a look of sympathy. 'If you had opened fire, the French would have swarmed all over you. You and your men would now be dead. So, as much as I value your keenness for killing the enemy, it can wait another day. And believe me, Captain, there will be many more opportunities. Besides, who else will fix my guns?'

'But, sir-'

'You live to fight another day!' Rai said firmly. 'Many others do not, so embrace that gift.'

Crestfallen, Cotton glanced at the bodies. 'I will, sir.'

Rai puffed on a cigar. 'Good,' he plucked it from his mouth, 'and perhaps you can tell me how the French knew we were here?'

'Sir?'

'They came here under,' he paused, teeth dragged a small portion of beard across his bottom lip, 'how do you say it? Cloak and dagger. Yes? So they knew we were here.'

Cotton chewed on his bottom lip. 'Agreed, sir.'

'So someone alerted them?' Cadoc cut in, eyebrows arched. 'Or more than one did.'

'Were they after the firearms I brought?' Cotton asked, half-disbelieving it.

Rai shook his head. 'No.'

'What about your inactive guns?'

The colonel looked up at the barn. 'No, not them either. They wouldn't know of them. No. They did not come here risking their lives to spike inoperative cannon. I overheard one of them say, 'Find him! He's here!' They came here for one purpose.'

Cadoc spat on the dusty ground. 'You, *senõr*,' he suggested.

'What? They came to assassinate you?' Cotton could not believe it.

'And they failed,' Rai grinned. 'For that small mercy, I will find out the truth. Come with me now.'

Cotton glanced nervously at Cadoc, because the partisan leader beckoned them to a house where once the door shut behind them, agonised and tormented screaming pierced their ears.

****

The one seated on the left was a sous-lieutenant and the other just a trooper. Both had their hands tied behind their backs, and both had been beaten severely.

'Do you speak French, Captain?' Rai asked Cotton who nodded. The tiny room smelt of dry grass and goat. Two sparrows flitted up in the rafters. The house was typically split in two; one for the owner and the other for the beasts. 'Mine is not very acceptable. Ask the officer who led them here last night?'

Cotton cleared his throat. He felt himself being drawn even further into the murky world in which Kyte had evidently been part of. Still, he also believed he should have played a bigger part in the night attack. He rattled off quick French to the man with bruised cheeks and lips that were split and oozing. The reply came as speedily back. 'He says *chef-de-battalion* Helterlin, sir. That will make him a major in our Army.'

Rai stared at the young man. 'What is his name?'

Cotton asked him. 'Tobias Woitsche, sir.'

'Doesn't sound French?'

'No, sir. He's actually from Hesse. He's German.'

Rai waved a hand dismissively. 'Another godless foreigner in Spain,' he said carelessly. The patriot known as Sebastiano, a short man with bushy, unkempt eyebrows and well-muscled forearms, prowled behind with bloodied fingers. He spat onto the floor, a string of it glistened in his beard. 'Ask the lieutenant what their mission was.'

Woitsche, with a slashed cheek from a musket ball, and two loose teeth from his capture, licked his lips. 'May I have water, please?'

Cotton asked and Rai shook his head. 'When he answers the question.'

The German, perhaps twenty, turned to his left as if seeking approval from the trooper in the hope that he would not be accused with cowardice, but the man had simply buried his neck in his chest

51

as though he had given up all hope of a reprieve, so Woitsche continued. 'We were sent to find someone.'

Sebastiano cracked his knuckles, a sound that made Woitsche shiver.

'Who?'

'I don't know.'

'Are you sure?'

Woitsche nodded confidently that what he was about to say would suffice. 'Yes. I was not told.'

'I think you do know. Let me tell you anyway: you came to get me. And this whoreson Helterlin sends just a detachment?' Rai gave a sarcastic laugh. 'He mocks me! He should have sent his entire regiment. And you know what? We would have murdered the dogs all the same.' He stared into the terrified German's eyes. 'Tell me where you are garrisoned. What is your strength?'

'We're a mobile unit. On the move all the time. We...' his voice faltered.

Rai waited for the translation, paused to reflect it, and gave a short determined nod to Sebastiano who was relishing the chance to inflict damage. He grabbed hold of the lieutenant's hair with his left hand and punched Woitsche in the face with his right. The blow was powerful enough to knock the German backwards in his chair onto the earthen floor, so extraordinarily powerful, that Sebastiano was left holding a handful of hair. The Spaniard chuckled at the find, let the strands fall away, and then reached down to haul the prisoner back up. Blood was pouring from his shattered nose, but the assault did not relent. It became harder because the Spaniard seemed to revel in it. He knocked the air from Woitsche, bubbles and pink foam frothed from his open mouth as he fought to scream. Fists swung in from left to right, short, close hits that brutally pulverized the officer until the screams fell silent and he lost consciousness. Rai allowed Sebastiano to continue. The hammer blows pounded flesh to jelly and splintered ribs. He went on punching so that Woitsche's head flopped with every strike. The trooper had not moved, or reacted to the sounds of the lieutenant's muffled cries as his face was repeatedly battered, or the blood that spattered his own green jacket.

When he had finished, Sebastiano took off his white sweat-soaked shirt, rubbed his knuckles and wiped them on the lieutenant's coat. There was the strong copper tang of blood in the air. Cotton looked absolutely terrified and sickened.

'You wish to give a better answer?' Rai then asked the other.

The trooper stared into his eyes, before spitting a mixture of blood and spittle onto the floor in defiance. Sebastiano growled.

Rai laughed mockingly. 'For that you will go straight to the knives.' He made a gesture with a hand and two of his men dragged the dragoon away outside.

'Where are you taking him?' Cotton enquired.

'To his death, Captain. That is all you need to know.'

Woitsche gasped loudly. He groaned, blood seeped out of broken nose and split lips to hang in thick tendrils from his chin. He gurgled something.

'What did he say?' Rai said to Cotton, but the captain was transfixed at the Frenchman's terrible injuries. His face was unrecognizable; swollen, pulpy and broken. 'Captain! Captain!' That got Cotton's attention. 'What is he saying?'

Cadoc felt for the young Ordnance officer. 'Just ask him, sir,' he said with sympathy. 'And this will all be over soon.'

Cotton leaned in, but could not bring himself to look into the bloodied horror of his face. He had never seen such ghastly wounds before and a creeping sourness was spreading up from his stomach to his throat. He gulped back the nausea. Woitsche spoke in short rasps, but they were merely wordless whimpers of pain. Cotton spoke to him again and listened intently to the German. It was only when he fell into silence that Cotton returned to his upright position.

'Well?' Rai enquired.

Cotton cleared his throat. He swivelled around to face Rai. 'He said that a guerrillero rides with his regiment.'

The Spanish colonel staggered as though he had been hit by a roundshot. 'What?'

'He is the one who told the French of our position.'

Cadoc gaped. 'He must be the betrayer that Captain Kyte tried to warn us about.'

'Yes,' Cotton nodded gravely.

Rai snarled. 'Who is the traitor? I want a name!'

Cotton looked grave. 'The lieutenant doesn't know, but he does know that he carries a rifle: a Baker rifle.'

Rai slowly turned towards Cadoc, eyes dark with fury.

****

The guerrilleros numbered sixty. All were equipped for battle and rode their horses under a sun-blazoned sky.

Fields of wheat shone like gold in the sunlight as the men cantered along a dusty road north. They rode beside gullies of yellow gorse abundant with bird nests, ravines and rolling hills, then took their mounts across hay meadows almost ready for the scythe.

'I shall find the traitor,' Rai said, a cigar hanging out of the corner of his mouth, 'hang him, disembowel him and afterwards, burn his corpse to ash. The enemy shall hear of the man's deception and his death all the way from Santiago to Cádiz.'

Cadoc, riding on his flank, cautioned his commander. 'We must tread carefully, senõr. If there is one betrayer, there could be another. How well do you know Saturnin and Dantel?'

'I know them well enough,' Rai explained. 'Have I told you of my time in New Granada or The Kingdom of New Spain?'

'No, senõr.'

Cigar smoke dribbled away from Rai's mouth. 'You are lying,' he said with a knowing smile and laughed. 'They were with me in the colonies for eight years. They are like my brothers. I trust them. Unconditionally. During the long years of garrison duties, we put down several revolts from the natives, fighting side-by-side. We even destroyed a British schooner who had wandered too close to our forts.' He glanced at the Welshman to see if there was a reaction at the said defeat.

The Rifleman was too shrewd to take the bait. Instead, he gazed up at the barren hills where a stand of pine trees were dark against the sky. For a brief instant, Cadoc thought he could see a figure standing in between the trees, but, as he continued with the journey, he could not be certain of what he had seen.

'When you looked at me earlier, senõr,' Cadoc said, 'I thought you perhaps considered I was the traitor.'

'Of course not.' Rai snapped, and shifted uncomfortably. 'I just think that a rifle in the wrong hands can do terrible damage.'

'In the right hands too,' Cadoc said with a grin. 'It's a bloody good job the French don't use them.'

54

Rai grunted. 'I couldn't agree more with that statement.'

'However, it would be easier if you'd let me go after the man,' Cadoc suggested. 'I'll put a bullet in his heart.'

Rai watched his friend. 'I've never doubted your skill, but *I* will kill the *bastardo*.'

They cantered along narrow tracks, away from the main thoroughfares, to keep away from the French cavalry patrols. By dusk they had reached a series of escarpments that obliterated the eastern and northern skyline. The track twisted its way up through the rocks, to where, partisan sentries watched them guardedly. There was the sound of a flute playing; its melody, soft and mournful. Cadoc could see a large cave smeared with dull orange light and yet more figures standing outside with muskets. Rai called up at the guards who wore cloaks slung across their shoulders, shared a joke, and allowed further up into the pass. There was enough space to leave their horses, so Rai took Cadoc, Sebastiano and Padre Tos, whilst the rest waited with their bivouacked countrymen.

Two men greeted Rai, clasping hands and hugging like kinsmen. Cadoc understood these were the colonel's friends. Saturnin was a brute of a man, bearded, hugely muscled and squat like keg of beer. He was in his late forties, and gave the Rifleman a bear-hug of an embrace before thrusting a wineskin into his belly. Dantel was a slim dark man who reminded Cadoc of Fito; cold-eyed, and calculating. He greeted the others warmly, but purposely blanked Cadoc.

As they ventured up a muscle-burning climb into the lip of the cave, and as the firelight smeared their faces orange, Rai whispered to the Welshman. 'Forgive Dantel, *amigo*. He distrusts anyone who is not from Castile.'

Cadoc allowed a quick smile to soften his face, but he knew his friend was being genial. The truth of it was that Dantel despised anyone who wasn't Spanish and Rai was being polite. The Welshman stared north in awe at the distant peakless mountains of Zamora, because he had never seen such a thing before in his life. They looked like strange islands rising above a vast sea. The red sun was gently falling away to plunge the land into darkness.

The men ate a stew of goat, beans, bread and consumed wine by the skin. There were perhaps twenty of them, all fierce-looking and united in their oaths to destroy the French. After the meal, they drank and small talk changed to that of Navales. Rai spoke of Cadoc's skill and was rewarded by favourable grunts and nods. Dantel remained impassive.

Saturnin spoke to Rai, but Cadoc saw that he was looking at him. Rai turned to the Welshman. It all went quiet. 'He wants to know why you wear a green coat instead of the usual British red?'

The Spaniards chuckled when the translation was given. All eyes were on him. Cadoc fingered his beloved patched coat. 'I enlisted in a redcoat battalion before joining the Rifles.'

Rai translated and Sebastiano to his left mimicked firing a rifle. 'He wants to know why green? Have they run out of red dye?'

Cadoc ignored the round of chattering playful merriment. He stared up at the twisting tendrils of tobacco smoke above their heads. 'It's for camouflage, and it works damned well.'

The men nodded, apart from Dantel who sighed as though he was bored. The fire crackled and spat and Cadoc watched his eyes flare angrily when his gaze crossed the Welshman's. He could not hold the gaze and the Spaniard looked away.

Saturnin asked if it was true that all British soldiers were convicts, thieves and murderers. Cadoc tried not to show offence, so played with the ends of his moustache.

'Some join up because it is better than being unemployed and starving. Some join wanting adventure, or patriotism.'

'What about you?'

'It was either join up, or get bloody married,' Cadoc said.

The guerrilleros exploded with laughter and passed around blocks of tobacco for pipes, cigars and flasks of brandy. There was a piercing scream coming from somewhere outside. No one reacted and Cadoc went utterly still. The moon was a silver blur behind drifting clouds.

'Dantel's men captured a French courier earlier,' Rai expounded cheerfully. 'He's just helping them with enquiries.'

Cadoc glanced at the Spaniard but his expression was unreadable. *Poor French bastard*, he thought. A horrible death awaited the messenger.

A boy no older than ten came to the fire wearing a French shako on his head. One or two men laughed, but Saturnin, cuffed the boy around the head like a bear swatting a salmon out of a river. The boy began to sob and the big man leant over, kissed his face and sent him away with a hunk of bread.

'He doesn't like us to mimic the enemy, especially his sons,' Rai whispered to Cadoc. 'One of his men once wore a French coat and was shot by mistake. He didn't die, but my old friend fusses over his children like a mother hen.' He laughed.

Saturnin, picking meat from between long, yellow teeth with a knife, spoke in a deep booming voice. 'The French will come back to Navales once they hear of the defeat.'

'I expect them to,' Rai said. 'That is why I called you here the moment I could. I have men watching the roads from Salamanca and from Alba de Tormes. There are only two other available routes to Navales. One is a poor road, heavily rutted with deep holes and the other is sunken. If the French choose that road, then they are as stupid as they are ugly. The banks either side are steep, wooded and rocky. A hundred men could block it and hold off an army there. They will not choose it. They will take the other road.'

'We will be ready for them,' Saturnin vowed, relishing slaughter. He was grinning, the corners of his eyes creasing like a crow's foot.

Dantel got to his feet, raising a drink. 'For Fernando and for Spain!'

The men cheered and cursed the French.

And so in the morning, long after the wives danced with castanets and tambourines, and the sound of the music had faded, the guerrilleros watched the bare roads for an enemy to come.

****

Two days later and there was no sign of the French.

Rai rode to all the sentinels who reported inactivity. Only goat herders, shepherds and the occasional peasants were spotted. Nothing stirred and Rai was anxious.

'Maybe they won't come?' Sebastiano suggested. 'They are cowards with no honour. They were beaten and do not want another hiding.'

'They'll come,' Cadoc told him.

'If there's one thing I've learnt,' Rai said, 'is that the French do not give up without a fight. They'll be back in greater numbers. They can't afford a defeat in one of the towns. News will spread and they need to quash the resistance. They will come.' He thumped a fist into his hand.

Sebastiano, his brutal face twitched fretfully, ran calloused fingers across his chest in the sign of a cross. 'Dear God, *senõr*. What of the people there? We will draw the heathens' attention. Soon there will be thousands coming to Navales!'

Rai waved away his concern. 'I have already taken care of that problem,' he said, soothing the usually violent man. 'They are all safe. Trust me.'

'They'll come after us, *senõr*.'

'Good. Let them. Remember: a wise wolf hides his fangs. We'll be ready for them.' He smiled one of his long white-toothed grins and slapped Sebastiano on the arm. 'I want our men alert. I want to know if one of them sees hide or hair of a Frenchman.'

'*Sí, senõr*.'

'Colonel!' It was Padre Tos who interrupted with an excited shout. He was riding a fast horse, armed with a musket and an ammunition belt clipped around his brown robes. 'Colonel!'

'What is it, Padre?'

The priest was smiling. 'The French are here. They chose badly.'

****

Rifleman Cadoc whistled the tune of Over the Hills and Far Away, before switching it to Spanish Bride when he thought of Edita; the girl who turned his mind to smoke with her beauty. He thought of her nakedness, her soft skin, her dark curls and the shadowed lines of her muscles in the morning's half-light. She was strong, graceful and feminine. He felt the familiar pang of love.

Rai began to sing a song, his voice was soft and Cadoc noticed a glint at his eyes. The colonel finished it and laughed away the tears of happiness.

'What was it about?' Cadoc asked him, then cursed his curiosity.

The Spaniard stared down at the empty track. 'It is about a love that cannot be spoken because of such heartache.'

Cadoc knew that Rai was still mourning his wife and children. 'I understand, *senõr*.'

Some wounds were too deep.

Rai smiled, and wiped his cheeks of tears.

Cadoc had oiled his rifle, screwed a new flint in place and had given the barrel a clean. He traced a finger along the walnut stock amazed at all the scrapes and knocks it had sustained over the years when a shadow loomed over him. He looked up. It was Dantel.

'Are you scared, Rifleman?' he said in English.

Cadoc smelt sour wine on his breath. He ignored the Spaniard and his needling words to stare down at the road where two butterflies danced above a patch of pale blue flowers.

Having his words disregarded seemed to make Dantel angry. 'You shouldn't be here. You aren't needed and you aren't wanted.' His voice travelled and several partisans turned to stare. Rai watched, but kept a polite distance.

Cadoc hawked and spat over the edge of the embankment. 'I don't care what you think. I kill Frenchmen. That's all that matters.'

Dantel shook slightly. 'You have no right to ride with us. This is Spain's war, not yours.'

'Your war?'

'Yes, my war,' Dantel said defiantly. 'I have fought in almost every major battle for my country.'

'So you fought at Ocaña and Alba de Tormes, did you?' Cadoc sneered, knowing that the Spanish defeats would needle him.

The slim Spaniard stiffened, but said nothing.

'Let me see now,' Cadoc continued, as sweat dripped onto his stained collar, 'you lost Seville, Granada, Córdoba, Málaga and Jaén, at the start of this year. Followed by Astorga, Ciudad Rodrigo, Lérida, Tortosa, Badajoz and Tarragona.' Dantel's face twitched with ire and Cadoc grinned at the intended impudence. 'The only places left under Spanish control are the mountains of Galicia and Cádiz.'

'You English think you're so righteous,' Dantel spat.

Cadoc sighed. 'If you're going to insult me, at least give it some proper thought. I'm Welsh, not English.'

The Spaniard shrugged. 'I don't care where you're from. You're another heathen foreigner in my country.' He eyed the Rifleman up and down.

'A heathen foreigner fighting for your country, don't forget.'

Dantel ignored the rebuke. 'Has Rai told you anything about me?'

Cadoc was tempted with more insolence, but bit it off in time. 'Not much.'

'I was at Buenos Aires,' Dantel ventured, eyes searching for Cadoc's thoughts as he went still. 'Yes, that's right. Rai told me you were there, but I don't remember you. You were just one man of a foreign invading army. And what was it? Three years ago? But there was one incident that I have never forgotten.'

Cadoc glanced back at Rai who was listening intently. By the looks of his face he had not heard his friend speak of this before. 'Go on,' the Welshman said, still prone.

Dantel's eyes ravished Cadoc's uniform. 'I never forgot the colour of your coats. Green. Dark green. And a man wearing such a coat beat and raped a Spanish wife of a friend of mine.'

Cadoc had known scores of men who were rapists, and men who had escaped punishment to enlist instead. 'I'm sorry,' he could only think to say.

Dantel spat onto the ground. 'I care not for your pathetic regret. The woman could not live with herself and took her own life. As a Catholic that is a terrible sin. Shame and guilt destroyed them both. All because of an *Inglés* soldier sent to that city by a greedy and corrupt government. I found my friend hanging on the day your generals surrendered. He killed himself over grief. I have not forgotten it and I never shall. You *ingleses* are a pox on this earth.'

Cadoc stood to full height, giving the Spaniard a sorrowful and thoughtful expression. 'I am sorry, despite your distrust of me. Our people were enemies. Once. I came here to help fight and I too have lost friends and companions along the way. How many unmarked graves have I seen from friends lost to a French bullet, a French sabre, or disease, or Spanish weather? I've lost count. I've even lost a loved one here. So don't tell me about loss, *senõr*.' His face changed to something brutal. 'Now I've no time for ill-mannered buggers like you. You address me like that again, and I'll knock you flat on your arse and send you straight to Saint James or any other buggering Saint this goddamn country has got. *Entiendes?*'

Dantel still glared at the Welshman, his throat emitting a low growl. He saw Rai stroll over, and strode away without muttering a single word.

Rai chuckled. 'You certainly have a way with words, *amigo*,' he said softly. 'But don't tell him I said that. If he asks, you tell him that I chided you and I've prayed for your sins.'

'He has balls like shrivelled plums.'

'I trust him with my life.'

'You're a braver man than me,' Cadoc scoffed. 'I wouldn't trust him with mine.'

'Dantel is a good soldier and a good friend,' Rai was enjoying the Welshman's anger.

'I don't care if he's a friend of yours or not,' Cadoc cracked his neck a couple of times to relieve the sudden antagonism, and rammed his black hat onto his head. 'If he speaks to me again, I'll hang the bastard upside down by his ankles until he chokes.'

The guerrillero leader puffed on his cigar and slapped the Welshman's back, before walking way. '*Bueno*!'

****

The enemy came at midday.

Sebastiano and three men brought news. A troop of dragoons led four companies of infantry, four canvass-covered wagons and another troop of horsemen protected the rear. Cadoc could see a smear of dust in the sky and considered the numbers of men, close to eight hundred. The French were coming in strength, but the Welshman decided that surprise would nullify the advantage.

'To your positions!' Rai instructed, and the men hurried to the high banks where they crawled and lay unseen above the sunken dirt road in soft grassy patches that rippled with the wind and weed strewn gullies. They let the French scouts go unhindered. These men were mounted on light horses and despite the imposing walls of the embankments, they trotted on without a care in the world. Rai had positioned his men with Dantel's men and Saturnin watched from the opposite side where the rocky edges were nearly double the height of Cadoc's position. Saturnin had a score of men, bristling with weapons that were ready to charge their horses from the wood on this side of the road to the scouts or use them to flee. Cadoc's plan was simple: kill as many of the enemy as possible, starting with the officers and NCOs.

61

He knew from experience that effective musketry could only be delivered at very short range; controlled and precise volley fire, not from each individual who skirmished. Smoothbore weapons were inaccurate and skirmishers, or men running about choosing targets, dallying, would never decide the outcome of a battle. The guerrilleros numbered one hundred and fifty. Rai had instructed the men, strung out all along the roadside to wait until the dragoons passed before starting the ambush. Only by surprise and one well-timed volley they might win the fight. Cadoc chewed the ends of his moustache in anticipation.

Hope for the best and plan for the worst.

Time went slowly.

Sweat dripped down Cadoc's spine. There were some animal bones nearby, yellowed with age. Shrew or mouse killed by a mink or marten. Soon there would be corpses and the beasts would have larger bones to gnaw. A shiver made the hairs on the back of his neck stand up. The sounds of insects buzzing equalled that of the hooves, marching feet and the squeal of the heavy wagons below. A nerve quivered in his gut and for the first time in months he was nervous. He glanced to his side. Rai was crouched over to his left, a young man with a gaunt face was praying. Cadoc could see a pulse beating along the line of Rai's throat. Carbines, muskets and rifles slid over rocks and grass. The Spaniards looked confident.

The French marched on, oblivious to the threat. It was certainly no Thermopylae, but it was an ideal choke point. The scouts had not signalled a warning, or the men were thinking of distant home, of their wives and sweethearts, or of food and drink. Whatever they were thinking, it wasn't death from above.

Like shooting rats in a barrel, Cadoc considered.

Rai took a massive intake of breath. 'Fire!'

One hundred and fifty bullets crashed out of one hundred and fifty muzzles.

The embankments were suddenly spotted with filthy powder smoke. Scores of French fell dead, and suddenly the packed column knew chaos. One minute they were a marching formation and the next their world had become one of screaming, blood and death. Horses whinnied and a man was kicked in the head, breaking his neck. A horse, shot through the neck, twisted and pitched onto an infantry officer who was on his hands and knees coughing blood.

The French commanders shouted at their men to fire up the guerrilleros, but as they sent protracted volleys, the Spanish pulled away from the edges and the bullets were wasted. They were like ghosts; one minute there, the next gone. A man was screaming piteously. The leading dragoon officer ordered his men to break out of the road, then to dismount to hunt down the enemy. He waved his straight-bladed sword high over his head.

'Now!' Rai shouted and from both sides men pushed and heaved logs and boulders over the edges. The noise was horrendous. The logs pounded the sides before slamming into the ground, creating a series of ear-splitting cracks as boulders and large stones smashed into the ground to send jagged fragments into the leading dragoons. A splinter, two foot long, struck a dragoon sergeant shattering his breastbone. An officer's face disintegrated as a rock rebounded up from the ground to crush bone. A white-eyed horse veered into another and both mounts fell, crushing their riders.

'Don't waste a shot! Make every shot count!' Rai ordered as though the strength of his voice would add to their destruction. 'Aim low! Fire!'

Cadoc shot at an infantry officer who was wearing his bedroll around his waist and shoulders. The bullet passed cleanly through his throat. Blood, bright as dawn, fountained from the man's open mouth. The Rifleman edged back out of sight and reloaded. Beside him, the young man was jiggling on his heels as he excitedly reloaded his musket. An older man with greying hair and dressed in a dirty white jacket and pantaloons fired and re loaded his wide-muzzled blunderbuss with a bag of nails. He had a dozen crude bags laid out in front of him. The pan flashed and the gun slammed into his shoulder, sending a blast of shrapnel down into the packed ranks which snatched two horsemen from their saddles.

The crude barricade of fallen logs was stymieing the French advance and Rai whooped derisively.

'I've seen tougher nuns! You boy-lovers! Your mothers are whores!'

The French infantry, mostly wearing campaign dress of sandy-coloured coats, brown pantaloons and covered shakoes, were trying to break free. They scattered, but the dragoons were in the way, unable to move past the obstacle. The infantry in the rear ranks were unable to pass or see the cause of the delay, instead had to endure the enemy's cheering and jeering over the sounds of Frenchmen dying. Saturnin's men sent more logs and boulders tumbling down to trap the horseman at the rear. A score escaped before the avalanche of timber and stone slammed down into the road. The wagons blocked the infantry's view. Some of the guerrilleros were firing at them, the canvass was pock-marked with bullets hoping to hit a powder barrel to make it explode.

'Fire!'

Padre Tos was there, firing and loading musket like a soldier. He had made a large cross from two lengths of wood lashed together, which he had pierced the ground with. 'God is with us!' he cried out. 'He loves us and will punish the French!'

The musket smoke was as thick as stew. The air blew hot, and the stink of blood mingled with the acrid powder-stench.

Pioneers, hugely-bearded men wearing tall bearskin caps and wielding great axes, pushed men out of the way to try to hack through the logs. Cadoc shot at one, but the man moved aside and the bullet passed through his thick apron. The French sent another volley upwards and Cadoc felt and heard the bullets whip the grass and ricochet from the rocky overhang. One struck the older man with the blunderbuss in the forehead. He grunted once, then crumpled like a puppet that had its strings cut. The embankments were clouding with so much gun smoke that it was getting impossible to see the enemy. The partisans just fired their weapons into the contracting, bleeding, shouting mass below, trusting they would hit something - anything to cause damage and pain. Blood spattered the roads surface and splashed up the banks.

Some guerrilleros, impatient and blood-crazed, emptied their weapons, before throwing rocks, knives and anything that could be used as missiles. A few over-keen stood too close to the edges, assuming that because the French were blocked, they were safe. The French still maintained volley fire and those Spaniards were whipped back. Cadoc watched one, stumble, and teeter on the edge, before falling down onto the French infantry, knocking down four bayonet-tipped men.

'*Vive l'empereur!*' the cry went up.

'Kill those bastards!' Cadoc shouted and pointed at the pioneers who were hacking their way through the blockade. Great chips of wood were flying through the air. Some of the infantry had skirted the verge and horses to haul the timber away. One pioneer with massive shoulders was breaking a boulder apart with a pick-axe.

Rai, clasping hands around his mouth, relayed the command across the roadside. Another Spanish volley hammered down at the barricade, flaying the French. But it was not enough and the dragoons were minutes from breaking free.

A guerrillero staggered with a large rock and, using all his strength, veins standing out on his thick neck, tossed it over the cliff's edge. Cadoc watched it plummet to crush two men into piles of convulsing gore. The Spaniards jeered the French dead.

The partisans kept firing through their own smoke and the blacker smoke of the grass fires caused by their own wadding. Cadoc looked for officers. He found one on horseback with a drawn sword who was bellowing at the men to reform their lines. The rifle cracked and spurted yellow-grey smoke. Cadoc twisted aside to see that the man had dropped his sword, a blood-slick hand was clasping his flank. A bullet immediately thrummed back through the air close enough for the Rifleman to feel the wind of its passage.

'Keep killing them!' Rai urged. 'Fire! Fire with every weapon at your side!'

Dead and wounded men and horses lay beside the road choking the ones that still lived. A few hollows in the embankment offered some safety for small phalanxes of infantry from the musket fire, but sergeants pulled men out and shoved them into files. The pioneer with the pick-axe still lived and more bullets thumped into his back, but he carried on breaking apart the barricade until Cadoc put a ball through the base of his skull. The pick-axe clattered onto the road, where French blood trickled.

Then, as the huge pioneer fell, the dragoons charged forward.

'*Vive l'empereur! Vive l'empereur!*'

'Back!' Rai hollered. 'Get to your horses! Back!'

Dantel, pistol smoking in a hand, waved his men back. 'Go!'

The partisans grudgingly broke their positions and hurried back down to where their mounts were tethered in a sheltered hollow. The sound of the French cavalry surging up the road shook the ground.

'Go! Go!' Rai kicked one of his stubborn men away.

'Let me kill more of them!' the man insisted and Rai slapped his face and pushed him forcefully away.

'Fool! You will not live if you stay! Now go!'

65

Cadoc waited for Rai and then returned with him to where the guerrilleros were hurriedly mounting up.

'Back to Navales! Back!'

****

The surviving dragoons formed up and followed the dust trail that whirled down the road towards Navales. The shattered infantry limped back towards the garrison at Alba de Tormes. There were so many wounded and dead that it was at first impossible to count them.

The dragoons were led by a man who had fought in the Italian campaign, crushed the Prussians at Jena–Auerstedt, destroyed the Russians at Preussisch-Eylau, and received the *Légion d'Honneur* for his heroics before being sent to Spain.

Chef-de-battalion Pierre Helterlin took his squadron to the Spanish village swearing an oath of revenge for the slaughter that had occurred. He would hunt the enemy down and burn down every settlement until they were caught and killed.

'These pieces of rat-shit have no honour!' he remarked bitterly. 'I'll gut them, their families, and their friends for what they did.'

And for the failing to capture the partisan leader, Colonel Herrero, Helterlin vowed privately. The Spaniard was a *Jean-Foutre*. Helterlin still fumed at his humiliation. He had lost good men during the night attack, and only one officer had returned alive. This was not how French cavalry - the finest cavalry in the world - should die. Cavalrymen should die with glory on the battlefield, not succumb to Spanish knives or Spanish bullets on night attacks or patrols.

The dragoons thundered after the irregulars and it seemed they were gaining on them. Fields blurred past. And then the road dipped to reveal the collection of tiled homes. Helterlin suspected that a few would hide in the houses, but leaving a detachment behind to seek them out, he would take the majority after the others who would be fleeing to the hills.

'*Capitaine* Jaillet!' he called to his subordinate.

'Sir?'

'I know this village. Take your troop around the western flank and I'll drive through it northwards. We'll pursue them on two courses. Leave a squadron behind to search the buildings.'

'Yes, sir.'

'We will crush them today. No survivors, *Capitaine*!' Helterlin commanded.

Jaillet nodded. 'Sir!'

It was then that Helterlin saw a puff of smoke blotting the ridge above Navales. Experience told him, that this was a cannon. But what were the partisans doing with artillery? He stared open-mouthed as a ball slammed into the road directly in front of them in a blur, bounced twice and Helterlin held his breath. It was all he could do. He heard the gun's discharge. It was feeble against the huge artillery barrage at Preussisch-Eylau, which seemed to cause ripples in the sky. He would never forget the sound; like peals of never-ending blood-seeking thunder.

The ball snatched the dragoon to his left out of his saddle, tore through the dragoon behind him, disembowelled the third horseman, and decapitated the fourth dragoon's horse, and suddenly men and horse of the rear ranks twisted, fell and collapsed screaming in blood, leather and steel.

'They have artillery!' someone in the ranks shouted the obvious.

Helterlin snapped out of his thoughts. No other gun fired. The guerrilleros must have captured a gun from a convoy, so he decided to continue the pursuit. The gun had caused damage, but would not fire again. The rabble would not have the skill of proper gun teams. 'We'll soon be out of range!' he called. 'I was at Marengo with the emperor! I charged the Prussian guns with Marshal Murat at Jena–Auerstedt! I charged the Russian cavalry at Preussisch-Eylau and I lived!' Spittle danced between his lips. He withdrew his sword, like most dragoons', the blades were made with the famed Spanish Toledo steel, and he held it high. 'I lived so follow me! And together we will destroy the Spanish dogs! Glory and France! *Vive l'Empereur!*' His men cheered him fervently.

Helterlin kicked his spurs on, leading the chase. His mare, captured like so many of his men's horses from the battlefields of Prussia and Austria, offered a gruff snort as though the beast understood the urgency. A great roar went up. The dragoons were filled with the mad, terrifying joy of the pursuit. The hooves of the

67

galloping horses beat a frantic and fierce rhythm on the Spanish earthen road.

The gun fired again and the ball tore through the air, this time going overhead. He wondered how they had fired so quickly because it was the same gun in the same location. He considered that the enemy were made up with the broken fragments of the Spanish army so may there may have had some ex-gunners. Nevertheless, Helterlin laughed sourly. His men were safe now and would corner the impudent gunners and hack them into offal. He glanced over his shoulders, his men as though reading his mind. The Frenchmen whooped and spurred their mounts at the partisans.

The road split and Jaillet took his men west. Helterlin could see the guerrilleros flee on their horses and they were closing fast. He clasped his sword tightly with his gloved hands, raised it in salute and kissed the blade. Retribution was as sweet as a virgin's first intercourse. He laughed. He would bed women tonight as he had done after every fight. There was something in victory that was exhilarating as sexual intercourse. He craved it, and he would look for it. After Marengo, he had bedded General Graf von Morzin's Italian whore who was trying to sneak through French lines. After Jena–Auerstedt, he slept with two Prussian women, one of whom was dressed in a Prussian grenadier's uniform. He laughed at the memory. After Preussisch-Eylau, he slept with a Polish countess who insisted her maids watch them make love. Spain had brought nothing but sullen encounters so far and what Helterlin wanted now was a Spanish girl. He didn't care how old or how beautiful. Victory would give him what he needed and with those thoughts that aroused him in the saddle, he did not expect to see a strange contraption blocking the road.

It looked like a cannon barrel lashed tight with ropes and blocks of wood and mounted on a hay cart. It dawned on him that this was an improvised artillery piece, cannibalised from parts and a big blue-coated man rushed out from behind a wall with a piece of slow-match.

Helterlin could not believe his eyes, and as he hauled on his reins commanding his men to veer left, the gun exploded sending grapeshot straight into the dragoons.

Helterlin saw flame, smoke and then nothing more.

****

'*Disparar!*' a voice shouted and thirty muskets flamed from walls, windows, trees and doorways. Dragoons tumbled from saddles from the volley, horses collapsed and they slammed to a halt as a line of guerrilleros blocked the roadside.

Capitaine Jaillet had heard the cannon fire coming from his flank, but assumed it had been the same artillery piece. *Chef-de-battalion* Helterlin had given him an order and so Jaillet would obey. His men were disorganised and he brought his chestnut mare to face them. They would form and cut their way through the brazen Spaniards. Tack jangled, scabbards clanked, men shouted and horses whinnied. Jaillet went to speak but found that he could not. His men were staring at him. He heard a distinctive crack above him and something was stinging his throat. Hot, salty blood erupted from his mouth. He was shaking. A trooper snatched the reins from his hand. Everything was moving slower, dizzying by sunlight flashing in his face.

'Reload!' someone was shouting in English above him, but Jaillet did not recognise the voice. Instead, he slumped forward, mouth taking in some of the horses flapping mane. He was very cold, limbs feeling heavy and he wanted to sleep for eternity.

Jaillet closed his eyes, welcoming it.

****

'Reload!' Cadoc bellowed, cursed himself, and then repeated it in Spanish. '*Recarger! Recarger!*'

He gazed down from the roof tiles, seeing the officer slump and the dragoons in chaos. A few of them snatched up their muskets and the balls smacked and whizzed harmlessly against the house. He cast a look across the tumble of roof tops to where Cotton's ingenuity had fixed two of the four guns in the short time the guerrilleros had been away. A crackle of musketry echoed and small plumes of smoke billowed to show that the dragoons were still present there. Another musket fired and the bullet cracked tiles to Cadoc's right. He lay back, reloading his rifle with blackened fingers.

The partisan line advanced rapidly and they shouted like most Spanish infantry when they did. They hefted an array of firearms, swords, lances and Cadoc even saw a boar spear waver in the air.

The dragoons were attempting to form. The enemy offered little defence against charging horsemen. Single line infantry on firm ground were a horseman's paradise. French blades would spill Spanish blood.

A shrill call echoed. The French turned in their saddles, thinking that it was one of their own, but the dragoon trumpeter wearing a white horsehair helmet and coat matching the colour of the trooper's facings signalled that it was not him.

Mounted guerrilleros thundered into the left flank of the French dragoons who reeled in shock. Colonel Herrero charged headlong into the green-coated enemy. One of his men even carried a Spanish flag tied to a lance and the point slammed into a dragoon who was trying to spur his mount away. The Frenchman was knocked to the floor, and the standard bearer rode the banner free.

Rai held his sword aloft. The blade, heavy with gold inlay, flashed in the bright sunlight. *'Fernando! Por Dios y por España!'* he shouted, drawing out the last word like a war cry.

For God and Spain.

Hooves pounded the ground, dust and clods of earth were flung high in the air. The dragoons were still milling and twisting when the Spanish cavalry crashed into them. Sword blades, pale as winter ice, chopped and thrust. Terrified horses screamed, hooves lashed and big yellow teeth bit. Swords clashed, ringing like smith's hammers. A Spaniard shot a dragoon in the face, then he was himself hit between the eyes with a French bullet. The enemy advance was checked. The dragoon trumpeter was sounding the call to retreat when Cadoc and more guerrilleros slammed into the French rear. Saturnin and Dantel's men had feigned retreat and as Cotton's guns splintered the Spanish afternoon's air, they had wheeled left and swooped up the hill to where Rai's mounted men had hidden behind a sloping vineyard.

Cadoc stood up so that the dismounted guerrilleros could see him. *'Disparar!'*

Perhaps twenty-five muskets and carbines fired from the line and more Dragoons, a mere forty yards away, were thrown backwards.

The Spanish then howled at the heavens and charged into the bloodied mess of men and horses.

There was nowhere else to go and the French knew that. Their only option was to fight their way to freedom. A few brought out their muskets and a smattering of partisans fell to their bullets, but they were being pressed from all sides. A dragoon speared a guerrillero's horse in the neck, causing its rider to haul frantically on the reins to control the beast. The Frenchman slashed into the man's neck and soon both were dying together, blood pumped bright onto the road. A pistol flared and a Frenchman grunted as he was hit in the chest. The dismounted guerrilleros reached the horsemen and they clubbed and hauled and stabbed more dragoons until a knot of blood-sheeted Frenchmen threw down their swords in the vain hope of surrender.

Cadoc scented victory and so decided to check on Cotton and the gun teams. He slung the rifle over one shoulder, jumped down onto a rain barrel as the murderous slaughter began. A dragoon drove his horse towards him and went to bring his sword down, but a bullet caught him in the flank and then screamed as Cadoc's sword-bayonet stabbed up into his belly, to be twisted and ripped free. The Welshman ducked as another blade sliced at him. This time from a man with epaulettes whose swordplay was quick and careful. The gleaming tip sliced open his forearm and a sliver of green cloth twirled to the dusty ground.

'You French bastard.'

Cadoc leapt forward to surprise the enemy, but the officer had expected the attack and the long sword almost cut him up through the chin. Cadoc ducked underneath the horse, sliced the stirrup's strap and pushed the man out of his saddle. The Frenchman managed to hang onto his sword. A guerrillero tried to bayonet him, but the officer got to his feet, slashed his blade across his face and the Spaniard fell away screaming, hands pressed against his face. Another partisan ran at him, slicing with his *cuchillo*, but the blows were easily beaten aside and the dragoon thrust once, the tip driving through an eye. The officer yelled, daring the enemy to come at him when a Spaniard on horseback put a pistol to the back of his head and the shot blew his brains out. Cadoc stared at the great glistening wound as the hair around it smouldered from the point-blank blast.

71

The Spaniards were fighting well enough and so he scrambled down the nearest alley. A dismounted dragoon saw him through the clouds of dust and powder-smoke and followed.

The sound of muskets firing still echoed but it was very sporadic, bordering on non-existence. Cadoc vaulted a wall, scampered through someone's garden. Roaming chickens clucked noisily and flapped out of the way. A spiral of thick smoke was rising higher. Cadoc saw streaks of blood bright on the earth. One wall of a garden was spattered with gore. A horse lay dead, its guts strung blue on the road, perhaps three feet from its corpse. A dead dragoon with no face lay at an odd angle on the street. Hooves thudded and men were shouting in English, Spanish and French. A musket fired and a man gasped. A carbine ball nicked the wall next to Cadoc, showering him with fragments.

'It's me, you dozy bastards!'

A man wearing a blue-coat of the Ordnance held up a hand in recognition. A larger figure behind saw him and shouldered his musket. Corporal Leatherby smiled like an executioner. Cadoc stared wide-eyed, heard loud boots behind him and threw himself sideways as the dragoon, shouldering his carbine, was shot through the body. Cadoc twisted, sword bayonet flashing in his hand to strike in case the shot had missed, but the sprawled enemy was bleeding and dying. The Welshman turned and sprinted to a low wall that was crowded with musket-armed defenders. One Spaniard hung over the stone wall, blood dripped from his open mouth. Dragoons were firing their carbines from horseback and from behind walls and houses. The hay-cart and the French eight-pounder were on fire. A Spaniard next to Cadoc was wearing a British Light Dragoon cap. He grinned back with tobacco stained teeth and fired his musket into the throng of the enemy.

Cadoc slotted his sword-bayonet to the loaded rifle and shouldered it. He aimed it at a sergeant leaning out from behind a wall, pulled the trigger and the Frenchman collapsed like a sack of old clothes. A Spaniard pounded the skins of a drum nearby until Cadoc shouted at the man to put the damned instrument away and pick up a musket. A small dog lapped at blood.

A carbine ball struck a partisan in the thigh and he fell back with a grunt. A helmetless dragoon charged with suicidal courage and was instantly flung back by musketry, blood jetting in a great fountain from his throat.

Cotton heard his voice over the din and ran over to him.

'My God, we've trounced them!' he said exuberantly. He wiped his blackened face, crossed with trails of sweat with his handkerchief. 'We gave them a drubbing they won't forget!' He ducked as a ball smacked noisily into the pock-marked stone wall.

'Well done, sir.' Cadoc thumped his arm and Cotton hissed in pain. 'Are you hit?'

'Took a bullet earlier,' he said as though it was all fault. 'Cornered by two of them. Shot one fellow with my pistol and Corporal Leatherby took care of the other.' Cadoc glanced over his shoulder at the muscled NCO who had joined them.

'Hauled the turd off his saddle and cracked him one across the jaw just like you would have done,' the corporal shouted. 'Then, I dashed his skull in with my musket stock.'

Cadoc was impressed. 'I owe you thanks for back there,' he said. The corporal waved a hand as though dismissing it. Cadoc inspected the captain's wound to find the carbine ball had passed through the flesh without breaking bone. 'We'll get that fixed up after this, sir.' He looked for more targets, but the dragoons were edging back.

'I think we did a good job here, wouldn't you say?' Cotton enquired, wanting praise.

The Welshman grinned. 'You bloody did, sir.'

'A pity the charge set the cart on fire,' Cotton remarked plaintively, 'but we only had enough grapeshot for one blast anyway. The Spanish twelve-pounder fires like a dream, though. I hope Rai keeps it. Still, we did well, all of us.'

They had done extremely well. The British and Spanish men jeered the survivors, shot their weapons in one final sporadic volley, and then clasped each other in celebration. Some pounced on the wounded and knifed, shot or clubbed them. Sebastiano, a man who beat other men to death with his bare hands, kissed Leatherby on the cheek and danced with tears in his eyes. Cadoc laughed, and lowered his primed rifle, because it was not needed now.

The ruse had worked, the French had been defeated, and Cadoc was smiling like a fool.

They had won, but there was still one more enemy yet to kill.

****

A single horseman took the steep rocky path up to where grey caves looked like fiendish maws. It was a high climb. When the peak was still touched red by the last daylight, the valley below would already be dark. There was no sound here, apart from the hooves and the slip of a rock which slid to drop over the side of the precarious path. The track was only wide enough for one horse, mule or men on foot to pass.

A gentle rain had fallen in the night. The wind freshened again and blew ripples across the puddles. The horseman, nostrils filling with cool air, brought his plain brown cloak closer to his body. A hawk circled in the bruised sky, gliding freely in the currents.

As the horse climbed to where the ground levelled, Colonel Antonio Rai Herrero dismounted and led his horse to the entrance to the largest of the caves. Four horses were tethered to a dying oak tree, the trunk a mass of rot and white fungi. He looped the leather reins around a boulder, then glanced at the dark outlines of the sheltered hills where a thin veil of mist still loitered to mingle with low grey clouds. Shadows were dark and the air felt crisp and brittle like the first days of autumn.

'Welcome, brother,' a lone voice rose up from the cave's gloom.

Rai turned and smiled as his brother stepped out to greet him. They embraced.

'You are well?' Rai asked him.

Fito smiled. 'Of course, and I am so glad to see you safe. I heard about the French attack and of your victory two days ago! A dragoon squadron smashed apart!'

'I had help, brother,' Rai said self-depreciatingly. 'It wasn't all my doing.'

Fito waved an admonishing finger. 'I hear it in all the villages. They speak nothing but praise of you. You won a great victory! You've made a reputation for yourself. I hear that El Medico wants to meet with you. What an honour!'

'The victory goes to Spain.'

'Our father would be very proud. I am proud,' Fito said, beaming. 'I want to hear more.' He clasped his arms around his brother's shoulders. 'I have the best French wine, our *aguadiente* and even some British Rum that needs our most urgent attention,' he said, breaking into a laugh.

'French wine?'

Fito grinned. 'Plundered two days ago from a supply wagon. I have crates of the stuff. It's rather palatable.'

'You like the taste?'

Fito frowned. 'It's a good wine,' he conceded. 'You know me I'll drink anything.'

Rai shrugged off the embrace. He walked towards the steep hills, expression of someone deep in thought.

'Brother?' Fito enquired of Rai's sudden behaviour. 'Is something wrong?'

'Do you remember the last time we met?'

Fito rubbed his unshaven chin. 'Yes, in Navales,' he said warily, knowing that his brother would have known the answer.

Rai looked down at the bottom of the gorge, face unreadable. 'The French attacked that night.'

Fito growled. 'I wish I'd stayed a little longer. My *cuchillo* would have found throats to cut.'

'And yet you left,' Rai said that sentence as a question.

'Yes?' Fito gave his brother a lop-sided grin. 'Where are you going with this?'

Rai was silent for a while. He gazed at the cave entrance knowing eyes watched him from within its cold darkness. 'Do you believe that Saint Teresa fought the devil here?'

'What Spaniard doesn't?'

'How many of your men do you have here now?'

'Two.'

Rai hoisted an eyebrow. 'Where are the rest?'

Fito scratched his neck with long, bony fingers. 'There are watching the northern roads. I understand that there is a large French convoy coming up from Ávila. Have you heard that the *ingleses* are falling back across the border?'

'Yes. It seems that we're going to have to save Spain ourselves.'

'I fear it won't be enough.'

'How so?'

Fito walked towards the slope's edge, where thick weeds grew amongst the rocks. 'We have no armies left. The guerrilleros are tiny against the French armies. It is said they number more than a quarter

75

of a million men.' He shook his head. 'We're a grain of sand against the tide. We haven't the firepower to defeat them. We haven't the manpower. We are running out of money. Half the partisan bands I know haven't horses, weapons or even the clothes to put on their backs.'

'We haven't been beaten yet!'

'Our regulars have. There will come a time when even the guerrilleros cannot win.' Fito stared out to the distant peaks, his face glowing by sunlight that had appeared through a tear in the clouds.

'Our people need to know the war is not lost.'

'It is only a matter of time.'

Rai growled, 'I never thought my brother was a defeatist.'

Fito was silent for a while. 'Not a defeatist, brother. I'm just considering the future prospects.'

'For Spain, or for yourself?'

'Both.'

'What about your kin?'

'What do you mean?'

'Do you see me in your future?'

Fito hesitated before answering. 'Of course. Don't talk such nonsense.'

'I think I'm making perfect sense,' Rai said. 'How long have you allied yourself to the French?'

'What?' Fito frowned in puzzlement.

'I never would have imagined this as possible. It makes my body tremble just to speak it and God forgive me for saying it, but you are a liar and a traitor. A better traitor than a liar, I grant you. I know when you are lying to me. I am your brother, after all. But why whore yourself to the French dogs? I think I understand. You've always worried about money. Land, money and titles. We are from poor stock and the French have taken everything else we had. We have nothing now except the clothes on our backs, the weapons at our side and the ground our boots tread on. But that's not enough for you, is it? You want more. You've always wanted more. And the French offered you that, didn't they? What was it? Riches? Titles?'

Fito shook his head and gazed at the horses that whickered softly. 'I think perhaps,' he said thoughtfully and carefully, 'that the victory has scoured the wits from your mind.'

Rai grinned wolfishly. 'The only thing that has been dulled is my sword. I need to sharpen it and work out the notches. It could so easily have been defeat.' He laughed sourly. 'Now I sound like you. But since the victory, one thing is certain; the French will come back to Navales.'

'They will.'

'But this time they will find it empty. The folk have long gone.'

'Where did you send them?' Fito asked.

'That is not your concern. From the moment the French dragoons attacked Navales, I knew it would not be safe for them to remain. But in truth, the French that night weren't after our people, were they? They came with one purpose and that was to kill me.'

'How can you be so certain?' Fito fiddled with the pommel of his sword, hanging at his hip.

Rai sighed. 'Because the dragoon major told me so.'

Fito did not answer. He just watched his brother, fingers fidgeting.

'*Chef-de-battalion* Pierre Helterlin was in a bad way,' Rai said. 'He suffered terrible injuries, but Doctor Escarrà worked his magic, and saved his life. Funny that, don't you think? He's an enemy of Spain, a killer of our people, and yet I made sure he lived. I prayed he would and God listened. Do you know what the Frenchman told me?'

'Go on?'

'He said that a Spaniard rode with him and his men. In fact, it was the same story that I beat out of another French officer. A Spaniard rode with them,' Rai said, shuddering as though the notion was too much for him to contemplate. 'He said that this traitor was employed to spy for him, to help root out patriots, name the leaders and have them destroyed. He said they would target the leader's families if they could not get to the man they wanted. What a despicable being that traitor is. And I think that our good friend Steven Kyte found out who it was only to get captured. But Steven was resourceful, even for a heathen *ingleses*, and he escaped.'

Fito glanced up to the horses again and Rai's eyes followed.

'I think Steven came to warn me, only to die by the traitor's bullet. A bullet fired from a British rifle I would imagine. Both the officer and Helterlin told me that my countryman carried a rifle.'

Fito turned his attention from the rifle holstered and strapped to his horse's saddle to his brother. 'You know the *ingleses* supply us with muskets and rifles. We both know the Baker rifle is a beautiful instrument of precision. They are highly valued and sought after. Many of our men carry them.'

'You carry a rifle.'

'I do. So what?'

'Not all of them are traitors to their country,' Rai said, catching his gaze. 'A traitor to his own brother! I learned that you had told the French I would be at Navales. They came to kill me because you had warned them.'

'Nonsense,' Fito said angrily and walked to the horses. 'I will no longer listen to your babbling.'

It was though Rai had been punched in the guts. 'I know in my heart it was you. You are no longer my brother.' Fito turned and Rai spat into his face. 'God forgive me, but you're a traitor and you're going to die.'

Neither man moved.

Suddenly, swords were whipped from scabbards and the two blades struck each other, the noise echoed down into the valley.

'Betrayer!' Rai hissed, spittle dropped from his mouth. 'My own blood a traitor!'

'I am no betrayer,' Fito exclaimed through gritted teeth. 'Is reason, intelligence, science and understanding cause for hatred? Our country is corrupt. The Church rules it. It is knotted in great tangles of superstition, ancient practices and suppression. Where is our liberty? Where is our free will? Why is it frowned upon to question our faith? The workings of the world? The French are free to do this, why can't we Spanish?'

'The French are invaders!' Rai gaped, incredulous at his brother's true thoughts. The blades were still crossed.

'They bring hope. They bring light.'

Rai's mouth twisted in rage, eyes a veritable blaze of hatred. 'They murdered my Ana! They murdered my children!'

Fito blinked. 'With progress there has to be casualties.'

'You bastard!' Rai howled and threw off his brother. He lunged and hacked with no great skill. The rising anger drove him on. 'You have no honour!'

The fight happened in a blink of an eye.

78

Rai barrelled into his brother with all the force he could muster, bringing his sword down at Fito's head in a great, bone-shattering attack. It slipped beyond the surprised Spaniard's guard, slicing a cut across above his left ear. Fito rushed aside, felt the wound and sneered. He brought his sword up sharply for the next assault. He did not wait long. Rai rained blow after blow at Fito's head, but each time he parried in a way that would have made a fencing-master proud.

And then Fito went on the attack, stepping in with sword high, tip angled like a silver snake, ready to strike. The sword flashed bright, darted and valley was ringing with the song of swords. Rai managed to turn the attack, chopped down, but Fito parried, back-cut, and turned the cut into a lunge that sliced deep into Rai's flank. He knew he had wounded his brother, for Rai stepped back, face grimacing and left hand grasping his ribs. Blood flowed through his fingers and began to darken his scarlet coat.

'Fate,' Fito sneered and Rai spat at him again.

Two men appeared at the caves entrance, both armed with muskets and pistols. Paz cocked the long firearm. Fito heard it, turned and waved them away. 'This is my fight,' he said. 'It won't take long.'

A crack seared the morning's air and the guerrillero next to Paz was thrown to the ground, leaving a small pink cloud in the air above him, made of blood and bone, which drifted an inch and then disappeared in the breeze. His musket spun away, clattering on the stone. The horses whinnied noisily. The weapon's mark still reverberated.

The three Spaniards were astonished by the shot, and stood momentarily dazed. They stared at the man lying on his front, limbs twitching. A huge, ragged, hair-fringed hole had been punched through his skull, leaving a glistening hollow of blood and bone. Paz, coming to his senses, wiped hot gore from his cheeks, before bolting for cover. He slammed into a boulder near the path's edge. He had seen a puff of jaundiced-grey smoke from the nearest hill where a line of stones ringed the summit. He took a lungful of air, then positioned his musket over the rock, aiming below the gun smoke.

Fito stepped back from his brother. 'Hold your fire, Paz! You don't have the range! He has a rifle.'

'I can see him,' Paz replied, seeing a figure creep east along the stones. A dark shape, but it stopped and the Spaniard gripped the trigger, made smooth over the years. The enemy was reloading. It would be an easy kill. The rifle shot was still echoing.

'Get down, Paz!' Fito ordered, glancing at the enemy marksman. From experience he knew the distance to be just under a rifle's effectiveness. 'Hold your fire!'

The man moved again and the temptation was too much. Paz pulled the trigger and the musket banged. He was sure he had hit his target, for once the smoke dissipated, he couldn't see the enemy. 'I hit him, Fito!' he yelled triumphantly. 'I killed the bastard! I killed him! I kill-'

The rifle bullet snapped Paz's head back with the impact, and the body dropped like a lead weight, blood spurting over the uneven ground.

'You son of a bitch!' Rai shouted at Fito, lungs-heaving with exertion. 'Fight me like a man! You French-lover! You French whore!' He was weakening, fast, but he would not show it.

Fito drove his sword down onto Rai's, using both hands, down to his knees, then kicked him over. Rai fell backwards, still holding his sword. 'It's a pity it has to end like this.'

'It hasn't ended.'

'Not yet. Stay here,' Fito said, ramming his blade into his brother's leg.

Rai screamed, more in anger, and slashed wildly with his sword, but Fito had gone.

The Spaniard ran to his horse and dragged free his own rifle. He used the horses for cover, concealing himself behind the oak. He primed the gun, then slowly edged out from the trunk, scanning the hills. The dead men's blood was steaming in the cool air. He heard Rai scream out his name, but he would deal with the Rifleman first and his brother afterwards. He could see the hidden marksman. He knew it was that bastard Welshman. He had seen the man's pride of the rifle, noticing that his clothes were grubby and ragged, yet the weapon's mechanics looked well-oiled, polished and maintained. Rai spoke highly of him. And he had earned Fito's respect and not many men had done that. But still he was an enemy and would die all the same.

A shape moved and Fito was tempted to fire at it, but considered it to be deception. He was too shrewd to fall for such tricks, having used many to send countless enemies to their unmarked graves. His brown eyes watched the man in the dark coat like a hawk watching its prey. An age seemed to pass, then the moment he had been waiting for. Cadoc moved and exposed his upper body for an instant as he attempted to get a better shot.

Fito's rifle cracked and he sprinted forwards out of the foul-smelling smoke to see the Welshman sag. The Spaniard let out an exultant cry! It was so easy! He was still smiling when he saw another figure slowly rise up from the crest to his left. The man was aiming at him. A cold shiver went up Fito's spine. He'd fallen for a ruse and there was just enough time for him to acknowledge his momentous and irreversible mistake with a smile of admiration when the rifle bullet hammered into his body, exploding his heart into bloody tatters.

****

A calloused hand gently gathered Rai to his feet. His crimson sash torn to stem the bleeding wounds was sodden, but the Spaniard put a grin on his pale face.

'I told you I'd put a bullet through his goddamned heart,' Cadoc said with a ironic smile

'How did you know I would come here?' Rai groaned.

Cadoc fussed over the wound to his side. 'I saw you leave, *senõr*. I remembered Fito asking you to meet him.' He straightened. 'I'm sorry he was a traitorous bastard.'

Rai shook his head. 'I can't believe he would betray me. Not my own brother.' He took a step forward and winced. 'Thank you for coming. You saved my life. Again,' he said with a wry smile, despite the pain. 'Who did you bring with you?'

'Corporal Leatherby.'

'I didn't know he's trained to use a rifle?'

Cadoc shook his head. 'He isn't. I brought him here with the rifle Captain Cotton brought with him. It's jammed, but Paz and your brother wouldn't know that.'

Rai looked puzzled. 'You used him as a decoy.'

81

'Yes.'

'Clever.'

Cadoc scratched his chin. 'Well, your brother shot him in the arm. Only a scratch.'

Rai grinned despite the pain. 'How did you persuade him to come with you?'

'A bottle of best *aguadiente*.'

The guerrillero laughed and looked down the path to where the hulking NCO waited for them. 'I guess there is only one true marksman here and that's you, Rifleman Cadoc.'

The Welshman was suddenly very proud and a pang of longing filled his mind. But for now there was plenty of rest ahead of him. Summer was coming to an end and the French were still marauding Spain, and so for now he would stay and fight.

****

Chef-de-battalion Helterlin woke from an agonised dream where sadistic men had sliced him with wicked blades, hammered bones until they broke and scalded his genitals with boiling water.

It was dark, wherever he was.

He tried to recollect recent events. His head felt like it was made of wool. He closed his eyes, remembering that he had been riding to a village. That was it. A village. But what was there? The guerrilleros. Yes. Goat-stinking peasants that had attacked him on that sunken road. Goddamn them! Helterlin's mouth curled into a snarl, then he saw flames. Flesh-searing heat and smoke. Cannon. Yes, that was it. A gun had fired at them. Had it hit anyone? Yes. Men and horses had fallen in chaos and death and blood. He could still hear the men screaming and horses whickering in terror.

He wanted move but he was unable to. Arms were stuck together. No, not stuck. Bound. He kicked his legs, but they were bound at the ankles too. His body throbbed.

Help me, he mouthed but no sound came out.

He remembered the questions voices asked him. It went on for hours or had it been days? Who was the Spaniard that rode with him? They repeated it over and over and Helterlin tried desperately to keep the name secret. But the pain became too much. He had revealed the one who was a true believer, or the *afrancesado*, the Spanish would call him, just to stop the torment.

And mercifully they did. He remembered thanking them, his hoarse voice turning into sobs.

Now his body was numb, but a terrible pain was lancing up from toes to his fingers. His eyes flickered, closed and opened into darkness. He knew he was outside. He could hear a dog barking faintly, a soft breeze on his naked body and the low murmur of voices. Where was he? What was he tied to? He moved his shoulder blades apart, feeling hewn wood and the clotted-wounds on his back opening up. Would they let him go now he had given them Fito's name?

There was the sound of footsteps. He turned to see who was coming but there was nothing there. Not nothing there, he could not see anything! He let out an anguished cry.

They have taken my eyes!

A man was talking to him. Helterlin had not bothered to learn a word of Spanish so had no idea what he was saying. The voice was spoken intimately, final and crisp. Helterlin heard the man walk away, or perhaps climbed down, for the footfalls sounded like they had been on steps. Something struck something below him, but what it was he did not know.

Then, there was a faint sound like the tearing of cloth and smoke singed his nostrils. Helterlin screamed. They had given him prayers and were now burning him alive! He was tied to a stake. He would die after all. His mutilated feet caught the flames first and he screamed and the flesh withered, twisted and bubbled. This was not how a hero of France was supposed to die! He shouted it out. He had been given a *Légion d'Honneur* medal by Bonaparte himself. He was a decorated hero of France!

But no one could hear his words anymore as the roaring, rippling flames reached his torso and Helterlin was burned alive.

****

The British wagons were loaded and two men watched the final canvass cover be strapped down.

'Has it really been two weeks?' Captain George Israel Cotton said. His arm was in a sling and he was fully dressed in his usual pristine coat.

'It has, sir,' Cadoc replied. He waved a hand to Corporal Leatherby who returned the gesture, even with a bandage around his arm.

'I still can't believe Leatherby went with you to safeguard Colonel Herrero! And nothing for his trouble,' Cotton said with a mystified look.

Cadoc had given the corporal three bottles of brandy and as many wineskins as he could take, and the wily NCO had failed to register that gift with his commanding officer. 'He's a good man, sir.'

Cotton raised an eyebrow to that statement, remembering their first encounter. 'It's funny how adversaries can become friends.'

'Aye,' Cadoc said and noticed that Cotton had held out a hand. He grasped it and shook it. He suddenly felt awkward, not knowing at first what to say. 'Thank you, for what you did here, sir. Getting the guns to work. A grand job.'

'It was nothing. You had all the right tools and my lads did the work, so full credit goes to them. I just got in the way.' Cotton smiled self-deprecatingly. 'I've been like that all my life. Getting in the way and not making much use of anything. I bought my lieutenancy and my captaincy without seeing or hearing a shot fired. I simply didn't do anything of merit and I guess that's what I'll achieve for the rest of the war. You can buy advancement, but not skill.'

'You led your men like any good officer could and you helped make a difference here. If those guns had not been fixed, we'd have lost. The bastard dragoons would have scoured us out of here and we'd all be dead. What we did here has already made its way to Madrid and I hope every Don hears about this. Back home they'd call you a hero. Here: you're an officer, a gentleman and a soldier,' the Welshman flourished a broad smile. 'Even if you don't think you are.'

Cotton hoped the burning sun hid his blushes. They were ten miles from Portugal's border, safe with Rai's partisans watching the horizon for enemies. 'If I wish to be a soldier, then I would wish to be a good one, to prove myself, not just for advancement.'

84

'You've done that, sir. You can go back with your head held high.'

'That's kind of you to say,' Cotton said.

Cadoc shuffled his feet. 'There is something else I wanted to say.' He licked his lips. 'I was hard on you when you first arrived. I assaulted you. If I still marched in the ranks, I would have lost my Chosen Man status,' he tugged at the faded-white stripe around his right arm, 'arrested and flogged. You reminded me so much of a man from my past that I actually thought he was here. I hate him and I couldn't see past my own hate.'

The 'what happened?' died on Cotton's lips as he decided now was not the time for the Welshman to speak of past horrors. 'I'd forgotten about that,' he graciously said instead.

'What I'm trying to say, sir, is that I apologise for my behaviour.'

Cotton smiled. 'I accept it. I do hope whoever this man is gets what he deserves.'

Cadoc's face creased into a sly grin that spoke of promised retribution. 'One day, sir.' The wagons and mules were waiting for the tall captain. Cadoc straightened his back to stand to attention and gave Cotton a smart salute.

The captain saluted back. 'Pass on my regards to Colonel Herrero. I hope he recovers. I look forward to hearing more of his exploits.'

'I will, sir. Where will you go now?'

'I'm being sent to Lisbon. You heard that we're pulling back. Not for long I hope. I'd like another crack at the Crapauds soon enough.' They both laughed. 'Before I go, you never did look into that trunk, did you?'

'No.'

'Take a look. You might find something that,' Cotton said, and the pause was significant and quite deliberate, 'you might be missing.'

Cadoc watched the retreating wagons and Rai's escort until they were gone. Then, the guerrilleros spurred back to their new hideout some one hundred or miles north-west of Salamanca deep in a land of lush forests, rocky hills, impassable gorges, beautiful waterfalls and sweet-smelling meadows. Rai's force had grown to one hundred and twenty men since the victory and more men were joining every day. The French still lingered so more were needed if Spain was ever to be free again.

Cadoc reached the village of Masueco where Edita waited for his return. She stood on the balcony of their new home, waving at him intensely as the partisans' horses clattered noisily in the small square that stank of spice-smelling, wood-smoke. The weapons that Cotton had brought had already been divided into working, to be mended and beyond repair, but the trunk had still not been distributed. He had commandeered it for personal use and it was still unopened. He raced upstairs, kissing Edita fiercely before reaching the trunk in the cellar, which opened into the village square. The floor was littered with bales of hay because he kept his horse there. He undid the clips and opened the lid. There were piles of boots, pantaloons, jackets and belts. His hands pulled aside a simple coat and his jaw dropped.

'What is it?' Edita called from the stairs. She then hurried down to the cellar. 'What does it mean, my love?'

'Everything,' Cadoc said, marvelling at the thing in his hands. 'It means everything.' He pushed open the rickety doors to let bright sunshine stream in. The light caught metal, which gleamed brightly in his dirt-ingrained hands. It was a badge showing a bugle horn.

He held the felt cap high with its green tuft and cord. Cadoc threw off his bandana and black hat and replaced it with the regimental cap. Smiling broadly with utter pride, because he was a marksman, and at heart, a Rifleman of the 95th.

Historical Note

Marksman is the fourth novella in The Soldier Chronicles series; a work of fiction, but nevertheless grounded in fact.

This story takes place during the Peninsular War (in Spain it is referred to as 'The War of Independence') at a time when the British had almost wholly withdrawn (apart from a strong Royal Naval squadron in Cádiz) to Portugal behind Wellington's ingenious series of fortifications to protect Lisbon, the Lines of Torres Vedras.

After defeating Marshal Soult at Porto on 12th May 1809, Wellington's army crossed the border into Spain, joined forces with the Spanish general, Gregorio García de la Cuesta y Fernández de Celis, and marched eastwards. On 27th-28th July, French armies under Joseph attacked the allies north of Talavera and were defeated. The victory had, however, been costly and, with Soult threatening to cut the road to Portugal, Wellington was forced to fall back.

By the end of 1809, the Spanish armies were crushed heavily at Ocaña and then at Alba de Tormes, while Sir Arthur Wellesley, now Viscount Wellington of Talavera, concentrated on the Lines. The value of these defences proved their worth (and cost) in the following year when Marshal Masséna led a French army through the fortresses of Ciudad Rodrigo and Almeida in a fresh attempt to re-take Portugal. Despite being repulsed on 27th September 1810 in his attacks against Wellington's position on the ridge at Buçaco, Masséna was able to force the allies to seek safety behind the Lines by his continued presence. However, he had no chance of breaking through, and a stand-off ensued until a lack of supplies and the imminent arrival of British reinforcements in the spring of 1811 led Masséna to fall back. But that is another year and by then, even after the victories, the war was far from over, and it had not even reached turning point.

In the late summer of 1810, when *Marksman* takes place, most of Spain was under French control, except that its army of over two hundred and eighty thousand men could not be concentrated. Three quarters of it had to fight against local insurrections, and contain and protect the supply lines from the Spanish irregulars - the partisans. Even messengers had to travel with an escort of sometimes as much as a regiment, or take the awful chance of being captured by the guerrilleros who would brutally torture and kill them.

Napoleon had been present in Spain, but left in late 1808. He ordered his marshals to achieve decisive battles against the regular troops, but was unable to grasp the power of the civilian's anger and the threat of the partisans. The Spanish villagers stubbornly refused to bow to the French. They burned crops, poisoned wells, and evacuated with all their cattle. Napoleon, having had his forces tied down, Wellington was thus able go on the offensive with the combined Spanish, Portuguese and British regulars.

The guerrilla forced the French into a terrible dilemma that they never overcame: how could regular troops fight against the enemy regular troops, while simultaneously fighting irregulars. Fighting on two fronts shattered the prestige of the French army, thought of as invincible, and it was ultimately a war that Napoleon could not win.

So why did they fail?

The French famously lived off the land, they robbed, stole and raped. Thus, they could never win over the civilians. There were those Spanish who supported French ideals and were a minority. Likewise, there were partisans who were self-serving, amoral and who terrorized their own people. But by invading Spain with the idea of forcing their own way of life and ideals, the French did not immerse themselves in the culture, traditions, religion and language. Instead, they violated the people and their principles.

During his exile on St Helena, Napoleon said, "the Spanish war has been a real ulcer, the first cause of the misfortunes of France".

It was not the killing-fields of Europe, or the disastrous campaign in winter Russia that ruined him, it was the Peninsular War.

And men like Arthur Cadoc fought in that conflict.

In 1800, The Experimental Corps of Riflemen was formed, becoming the 95th Rifle Regiment of Foot three years later. Abandoning the red coat, the Rifles wore the distinctive 'green jacket'; the British Army's first attempt at camouflage. Not only was the uniform and training different to that of the other line regiments, they were equipped with the finest firearm of the age: the Baker rifle. Accurate at 75 yards and capable of hitting a target at 200, the rifle, with its seven rectangular-grooved barrel, gave the regiment a distinctive edge over their French opponents. The Rifles were masters of the battlefield skirmishes, marches and were held in high-esteem by allies and foes alike.

Rifleman Cadoc is an invention, but I'd like to think that the ghosts of his regiment are pleased with his incarnation, and if I've done them justice, I can sit back in my chair a very proud man.

I'd like to thank Angharad Evans for her assistance with Cadoc's Welsh and Catherine Lenderi, my editor, who is not only completely and extremely professional, but she is one of the nicest people in the world.

I'd also like to praise Jenny Quinlan for producing a truly superb book jacket cover for *Marksman*. It's better than I could ever have imagined and brings Cadoc and his world alive.

For further reading I recommend reading Jac Weller's excellent *Wellington in the Peninsula 1808-1814* and David Gates' *The Spanish Ulcer: A History of the Peninsular War*. For the 95th Rifles, no other books come to mind than *The Recollections of Rifleman Harris* and Mark Urban's *Rifles: Six Years with Wellington's Legendary Sharpshooters*. This is an absolutely breath-taking piece of narrative history, tracing the regiments origin and achievements throughout the Peninsular War.

Arthur Cadoc's stories will continue.

17216271R00054

Printed in Great Britain
by Amazon